WHAT
AN ALTAR GUILD
SHOULD KNOW

PAUL H. D. LANG

CONCORDIA PUBLISHING HOUSE

Saint Louis, Missouri

To my wife
Flora Bade Lang

The filmstrip *Duties of the Altar Guild* **has been produced by
Concordia Publishing House to correlate with this handbook.**

Concordia Publishing House, St. Louis, Missouri

© *1964 Concordia Publishing House*
Slightly Revised 1968

MANUFACTURED IN THE UNITED STATES OF AMERICA

7 8 9 10 11 12 13 14 15 16 WP 89 88 87 86 85 84 83 82 81 80

CONTENTS

A good example of contemporary church architecture

Whatsoever things are true,
  whatsoever things are honest,
  whatsoever things are just,
  whatsoever things are pure,
  whatsoever things are lovely,
  whatsoever things are of good report,
  if there be any virtue and
  if there be any praise,
  think on these things.

PHILIPPIANS 4:8

PREFACE

This handbook was written to give information, guidance, and inspiration to altar guilds. It is based on many years of study and experience, especially in the study of liturgics and in helping women learn to do altar guild work.

To organize an altar guild is not difficult, but to teach those who have become members of the guild what they should know is not so easy. That is why a book on what an altar guild should know is desirable. It should help new members learn the basic things that are required of them, and it should serve to improve the work of experienced members and help them assist those who are just beginning. For all members of the guild, new and old, as well as for pastors, it should be helpful as a constant handbook for ready reference and guidance.

I want to thank publicly all who have assisted me in the preparation of this book: Ann Hesselmeyer, who directs the altar guild of Trinity Lutheran Church, Palo Alto, Calif., and who, together with Mrs. Richard Byers, did the typing; Evelyn Houseman and Mrs. Ernest G. Seaman, who suggested the illustrations; and Ann Hesselmeyer and Rev. Norman C. Theiss for reading the manuscript.

May this book serve the greater glory of God.

PAUL H. D. LANG

The Feast of the Annunciation 1964

CHAPTER I

About Its Opportunities for Service in the Church

A Needed Service

The altar guild can make a needed and valuable contribution to the worship services of the church. It can keep the chancel and its furnishings clean, vest the altar according to the requirements of the days and seasons of the church year, wax the brasses, place the candles, arrange the flowers, and take care of the sacred vessels, linens, and vestments. It can make a study of the externals of the church's worship so that it knows what is traditionally appropriate and desirable. It can devote itself to the fine art of church needlework and learn to make and embroider the sacred linens, paraments, and vestments.

Beautifying Worship

The service which the altar guild can render is valuable as an aid to extol the beauty and greatness of God and to awaken the response of His people in all forms of beauty, care, and reverence. Beauty in the church is not a matter of indifference. God gave special instructions for beautifying the tabernacle and the temple and their services in the Old Testament (Ex. 25—27; Num. 4; 1 Kings 5—7; 2 Chron. 3, 4). A similar concern is evident from a prime principle of worship in the New Testament: "Let all things be done decently and in order." (1 Cor. 14:40)

Why do we want to make the house of God and our worship of God as reverent and beautiful as possible? Such a desire is of God and for God. He is present in our churches. Through His Word and sacraments, Christ comes to us as we are gathered together in His name. He speaks to us, and we speak to Him. He gives to us, and we give to Him. God is present. As women make their homes as beautiful as possible for their loved ones, so we, loving God above all things, want to make His house and our worship of Him even more beautiful than our private homes. Whatever we do in humble and adoring faith to achieve this end is a distinct service of love.

Preparing a Setting for the Gospel

By making God's house and the services of the church more beautiful, we provide the Gospel a setting in which it is more attractive to people and puts them in a more receptive frame of mind for worship. We understand the allure of beauty in other areas of life. A dinner served with fine tableware, candles, and flowers on a beautifully set table is more appealing and even tastes better than one served in pots and pans on bare boards. A diamond is more attractive when mounted on a handsome ring than when lying in a diamond cutter's drawer. Of course, God's Word and sacraments are not dependent on human embellishment for effectiveness. They are in themselves "the power of God unto salvation to everyone that believeth" (Rom. 1:16). It is only fitting, however, that we should present them in surroundings that are as attractive as we can make them. Perhaps we have failed to attract, even alienated, some people by being indifferent to the setting in which we present the Gospel and by tolerating crudities and vulgarities in our churches.

A Spiritual Service

The service which an altar guild can render is not only practical but also spiritual. The practical side is to learn about liturgical colors, the use of candles, Christian symbols, and the like. It includes the work of sewing, washing, and polishing to keep the chancel in proper order and condition. But these labors are only means to an end; they aid the faithful in worship. Worship remains the all-important thing.

Members of the altar guild may consider themselves stagehands in the house of God. They take posts behind the scenes to do the staging for the church's worship. Their work is related to the spiritual life of the congregation. Someone has said that the altar guild is to minimize the work of Satan in the house of God. It is well known how the devil likes to get into holy places and mishandle holy things. He likes to distract Christians especially when they are worshiping in church. He has quite a bag of tricks with which he does this in the chancel. The work of the altar guild is to hinder Satan and help the church to worship. It is a work by which the Lord and the worshiping congregation are served. Therefore its real purpose is spiritual. The work is itself a worship, a "reasonable service." (Rom. 12:1)

Externals Not Essential

The members of the altar guild should understand clearly that God has not given Christians of the New Testament era specific laws governing the outward forms of worship. Christianity is not essentially a matter of externals but of faith and life. Strictly speaking, it cannot be said that a church is Christian because it does or does not have a beautiful service. Where the Word of God is rightly taught and the sacraments are rightly administered, there is the Christian church. Neither is uniformity in externals necessary for the unity of the church. Outward forms need not be everywhere alike. Therefore no church or church member should ever criticize or condemn another because one has fewer or more external rites and ceremonies than the other. With our Lutheran Confessions we profess that "it is sufficient for the true unity of the Christian church that the Gospel be preached in conformity with a pure understanding of it and that the sacraments be administered in accordance with the divine Word. It is not necessary for the true unity of the Christian church that ceremonies, instituted by men, should be observed uniformly in all places." [1]

[1] Augsburg Confession VII 2, 3 (from German text); *The Book of Concord: The Confessions of the Evangelical Lutheran Church,* trans. and ed. Theodore G. Tappert in collaboration with Jaroslav Pelikan, Robert H. Fischer, Arthur C. Piepkorn (Philadelphia: Muhlenberg Press, 1959), p. 32.

Externals Are Important

Nonetheless, externals are invariably associated with Christian worship. Therefore they are important. Christian doctrine, faith, and life are never merely theoretical, barren, or lifeless. They express themselves in outward acts. Churches formulate principles and policies also in matters which are neither commanded nor forbidden by God. These principles and policies are not based on any ceremonial laws of God, but on Christian doctrine, tradition, and sanctified common sense.

A First Principle

A first principle of worship is that traditional forms of worship are to be retained as long as they are helpful and in harmony with the Word of God. Those forms that become corrupted or lost may be restored and purified, brought back to their originally pious purpose. For instance, worshiping toward the altar in church is a traditional and laudable Christian custom whose purpose is to focus the worshipers' attention on the presence of God among His people, to remind them of the redeeming sacrifice of Christ, and to stimulate their sacrifice of self, their prayers, praise, adoration, and service to Him. If this original intention comes to be corrupted or lost, worshiping toward the altar must be purified of all corrupt, possibly idolatrous associations, but the altar itself is certainly to be retained or restored. The same principle applies to the other furnishings, rites, and ceremonies of Christian worship.

A Second Principle

Another principle is that everything in worship exalt God and bring His grace to man. Everything in worship is to aid the communication of the Gospel so that man may be attracted to it and, by the grace of God, be sanctified and edified by it. Nothing in worship practice should have the purpose merely of giving man pleasure, entertainment, or emotional thrill. This is idolatry. For example, a beautifully embroidered set of paraments serves to glorify God. It is not to glorify the members of the altar guild who made it, and it is not merely to give pleasure to those who see it. No matter how beautiful a thing may be, whether ceremony, music, architecture, or needlework, it has a rightful place in the church's worship only if it serves to glorify Him who has created, redeemed, and sanctified us. Everything that is self-willed, self-seeking, or self-glorifying is worthless and worse than worthless.

A Third Principle

Since God has indeed enjoined us to gather ourselves together about the Word and sacraments but has not laid down detailed laws concerning the externals of worship, we are not legalistic about the ceremonies which enhance worship in our own parishes. We do not insist: "This or that must be done," nor what is just as wrong: "This or that must not be done." As long as it is not a question of some ceremony or usage contrary to Holy Scripture, we neither criticize nor condemn one another for being "high church" or "low church," "Catholic" or "Protestant." All things that are neither commanded nor forbidden by God are humbly left in the domain of Christian liberty and are dealt with evangelically, never legalistically.

It is in the spirit of this principle that this book is written. The book is properly a source of information about those worship externals with which an altar guild should be acquainted. The ideas expressed in it are not to be taken legalistically. No altar guild should use it as a kind of Bible. It is not necessary to accept everything that is asserted or recommended in it. A book of this nature must be fairly comprehensive; otherwise those who have more ceremony than others will be left in the lurch and not find the book as helpful as it should be. Therefore also those things with which some readers may not be acquainted or with which some are not at all in sympathy are properly discussed. Each altar guild may select what it can use and disregard the rest. At the same time, it is by a judicious sharing of worship practices that the local worship setting may be enhanced.

For further study of the Lutheran principles in external matters, it is suggested that the altar guild look up such words as adiaphora, ceremonies, church, and the Mass in the index of the Book of Concord.[2] The author has learned from experience that it is best for members of the altar guild to make such a study for themselves. First, it helps them get acquainted with the Book of Concord; second, it gives them a better understanding of the Lutheran principles concerning church rites and ceremonies.

A Service Group

An altar guild, like the choir, the ushers, and acolytes, is a service group within the congregation. It is not a social club. Therefore dues, parties, suppers, sales, and all other money-making endeavors have no place in its program. Not the altar guild but the congregation is responsible for providing the money needed for linens, paraments, furnishings, and everything necessary for the church services. Just as the cost of the candles used in the services and the bread and wine for the Sacrament of Holy Communion is generally included in the congregation's budget, so the needs of the altar guild should be put into the budget. If this is not feasible, perhaps the women's society or some other organization within the church can supply the money for the things that are used in the chancel. The altar guild is not to be concerned about money. Its purpose is to serve by doing certain kinds of work. Let every member of the altar guild be impressed with the importance and dignity of this work and do it humbly to the glory of God.

Acceptance of Gifts

It is wise for the altar guild to ask the approval of the pastor before accepting any gifts for linens, embroideries, or ornaments for the altar and church. It is up to the pastor and the authorized officers of the congregation

[2] *Concordia or Book of Concord: The Symbols of the Evangelical Lutheran Church* (St. Louis: Concordia Publishing House, 1957); or an English translation based on a more critical text, the edition cited in note 1 above. Both may be ordered from Concordia Publishing House, 3558 S. Jefferson Ave., St. Louis, Mo. 63118, or from another Lutheran publishing house or bookstore.

to accept or reject any gift. If the pastor is consulted when gifts are proposed, unfortunate mistakes may be avoided. The purpose of the altar guild is to help the pastor and to work in closest cooperation with him.

Wisehearted Women

If these purposes of the altar guild and the principles concerning the externals of the church are clearly understood and properly carried out, the members of the guild will render a great service to the Lord and the congregation. They are the successors of the wisehearted women who helped furnish the tabernacle of God in the wilderness. Of them it is written: "All the women that were wisehearted did spin with their hands and brought that which they had spun, both of blue and of purple and of scarlet and of fine linen" (Ex. 35:25). They are the followers of Mary, Martha, Salome, and the other women who ministered to our Lord and His disciples. They are the pastor's assistants, who relieve him of certain work in the chancel which they can do, so that he can devote himself to other important matters. Their service is a beautiful and blessed one, a labor of love in the church.

CHAPTER II

About Reverence and Devotion

God

Since God is our Creator, Redeemer, and Preserver, we owe Him all the reverence we are able to give. He is present everywhere in His ongoing work of creation, and it is the duty of all His creatures to "stand in awe of Him" (Ps. 33:8). But He has appointed certain signs through which He is present in His grace by the means of grace "for us," as Luther puts it. These signs are His Word and sacraments. Christ also said: "Where two or three are gathered together in My name, there am I in the midst of them" (Matt. 18:20). There are certain places where we feel His presence more impressively. "How awesome is this place! This is none other than the house of God, and this is the gate of heaven" (Gen. 28:17). Such a place is the church, the house of God, where His Word and sacraments are administered and where we gather together in His name to worship Him.

God's House

The church is a symbol of God's greatness in love and grace, and therefore altar guild members treat the church as God's house. They keep the sacred place holy. When they go in, they walk reverently. They may genuflect and make the sign of the cross. They may kneel in prayer, adore God, thank Him, and ask His blessing on their work. While they are in church, they behave as well as if they saw God among them with their bodily eyes. They are quiet. They limit conversation to brief and softly spoken comments in reverence to God. They avoid doing any work in church that can be done in the parish house or elsewhere.

Sacred Things

Reverence for God also includes showing due respect for things set apart especially for worship of God. Uzzah was struck dead because he laid his hand on the ark of God, which the priests and Levites alone were allowed to touch (2 Sam. 6:3-8). The altar is a symbol of the presence of God. Every time altar guild members pass it, they show reverence to God by bowing the head. The consecrated bread and wine left over from the Sacrament of the Altar have participated in the sacramental presence of the holy body and precious blood of Christ. Those whose duty it is to dispose of them will do it reverently. They may put the bread into the ciborium and pour the wine into the piscina or on the ground at a proper place outside the church. They may pour away the water used for Holy Baptism in the same way. The sacred vessels and linens used in the administration of the sacraments come into direct contact with Christ's holy presence. When members of the altar guild clean them and handle them, they do it reverently. They express their reverence by the care they give all things used in the church's worship.

The Clergy

The pastor and the altar guild are fellow servants of Jesus Christ. But on account of the office to which the clergy were ordained, they are entitled to reverent respect on the part of the altar guild. "We beseech you, brethren, to know them which labor among you and are over you in the Lord and admonish you to esteem them very highly in love for their work's sake" (1 Thess. 5:12, 13). Pastors are God's representatives in the church. Therefore God requires that they be honored for their office.

The altar guild will always remember that it exists to assist the pastor. If differences of opinion or friction ever arise between a member of the guild and the pastor, she will respect the pastor's position and do his wishes. It is of the greatest importance that the altar guild work together with the pastor and be loyal to him for the office he holds. All the members will also work in harmony with one another. They will place the love of Christ and the peace of the church above personal feelings and opinions.

Head Covered

For women to wear an appropriate head covering in church is a custom of reverence according to traditions of the church going all the way back to apostolic days. Therefore a rubric in the service book says: "It is a laudable custom, based upon a Scriptural injunction (1 Cor. 11:3-15), for women to wear an appropriate head covering in Church, especially at the time of divine service." *

Devotion

Reverence and devotion are closely related in religious matters. Reverence is a feeling of deep respect for God, mixed with wonder, awe, and love. Devotion is a loyal, steadfast affection and consecration like that of the holy women who ministered to our Lord during His earthly ministry. Both reverence and devotion are primarily matters of our inner life and determine our attitudes, but they express themselves in our outward actions. Members of the altar guild will show their devotion in a number of ways.

Sacrifice

Altar guild members will show sacrificial love by being willing to give their time and service whenever it is needed, even if this means inconveniencing themselves. The spirit of devotion will make them willing to bring such sacrifices out of love to God and His church, not merely from a sense of duty. They will do their work "heartily, as to the Lord and not unto men." (Col. 3:23)

Dependability

Ladies of the altar guild will be dependable. If something unexpected should happen so that they cannot carry out their assignment, they will

* *The Lutheran Liturgy* (St. Louis: Concordia Publishing House, 1955 or later printing), p. 427.

17

arrange for someone else to do the work for them. Negligence in the work of the altar guild is a very serious matter. When the pastor and the congregation come to church, they expect everything in God's house to have been made ready for the worship service. They depend on the members of the altar guild to do their work faithfully.

On Time

Devotion also means being on time and doing the work at the right time. It is necessary for the altar guild to make the chancel ready in plenty of time, not right before the service is to begin. It is also important that the clergy not be disturbed when they are preparing themselves by prayer in the sacristy before the service. After the service the altar guild will wait till all the people have left the church before they enter the chancel to do their work. How important it is for members of the altar guild to be on time and to do their work at the proper time.

Thorough

In serving God the altar guild should strive to do everything as well as possible, thoroughly, and never carelessly or hurriedly. When they vest the altar, place the candles, arrange the flowers, and the like, they make sure that everything is proper, in its proper place, and orderly. They see to it that everything in the chancel is clean and correct. This requires patient and careful work. If the tasks are done hurriedly, almost invariably they will be done slovenly. But slovenliness has absolutely no place in God's house.

Informed

The spirit of devotion will make a person eager to learn more and more about the things to which he is devoted. Members of the altar guild will therefore seek to be informed. They will study the church services, for example, the Holy Communion service, the morning service without Communion, Holy Baptism, matins, vespers, the wedding service, and the funeral service, so that they may learn the necessary preparations for each service. They will also study the church year and learn how to prepare the church for the various feasts and seasons, such as Easter, Christmas, Advent, and Lent. They will study the significance and use of the altar, crucifix, candles, paraments, linens, vestments, and all other things used in worship. Everything in church worship has meaning and purpose. If things are done in a certain way, it is for good reason. The reasons may be theological, traditional, or aesthetic. Whatever the reasons may be, the altar guild will seek to learn them. Therefore altar guild members attend study meetings, read books, and train themselves to do their work properly and well.

CHAPTER III

About Membership and Organization

Membership

Since the women who serve on the altar guild deal with things sacred and divine, it is desirable to select only such women as are devout Christians and have time and talent to volunteer for the work. It is not necessary that they have previous experience, but a right attitude and willingness to learn are essential.

Some phases of altar guild work require special skills, such as sewing and needlecraft. Therefore membership may preferably be by invitation. It is better to select individuals according to their personal qualifications rather than on the basis of age or willingness to help. If it is necessary to ask for volunteers, be assured that willing workers will grow in aptitude and appreciation by their in-service training.

The altar guild is a working group which performs specific specialized services. Therefore it need not be large. Six to ten members are adequate for most congregations. The guild may be simply a committee of the women's society. However, even though it is limited in membership, it need not give the impression of being an exclusive organization. To avoid hurting the feelings of any lady who might wish to be a member, it is best to make it understood that no one is barred from membership. If someone wants to join even though she has not been formally invited, she may be given the privilege of membership and assigned the kind of work she is qualified to do.

Organization

The organization of the altar guild may be kept quite simple. Perhaps a formal set of "Rules for the Altar Guild" will be all that is needed. These rules may be approved by the congregation and altered from time to time as circumstances makes changes and additions desirable. The following rules may serve as a model:

1. The altar guild shall be composed of women communicant members organized under the leadership of the pastor for the reverent care of the chancel, the sacred vessels, and the vestments, and for usual altar guild work.

2. A director and a secretary-treasurer shall be chosen by the members of the altar guild in the first meeting after the First Sunday in Advent of each church year.

3. The director shall conduct the meetings and initiate, assign, and supervise all work of the guild.

4. The secretary-treasurer shall be in charge of all money and goods, keep such books and records as are needed for the work of the guild, and notify members of the meetings.

5. Regular meetings shall be held on the _____ of each month at _____ . Special meetings may be called by the guild director or the pastor.

6. The members shall take turns, as appointed by the director or as agreed by the guild, in doing the work preparatory for church services and after church services.

7. The general duties on the day before each church service are: to clean the chancel; to see that the altar brasses are waxed and that new candles are placed when needed; and that everything is arranged for the kind of service to be conducted (Holy Communion service, morning service without Communion, matins, vespers, Holy Baptism, etc.); to arrange the flowers; to wash and polish the sacred vessels; and to clean and iron the linens and vestments when necessary.

8. The general duties after each church service are to clean and store in their proper places the things used for the service and to see that the chancel is in proper order for the ferial, or week, days.

Office of Induction into the Altar Guild

The following office, to be conducted by the pastor in church with the members of the altar guild participating, is offered for the induction of new members into the altar guild.

✠   ✠   ✠

All shall rise, and the pastor, facing the altar, shall say:

In the name of the Father and of the Son ✠ and of the Holy Ghost.

The members of the altar guild and the candidate(s) shall say:

Amen.

℣: We wait for Thy loving-kindness, O God:

℟: In the midst of Thy temple.

℣: Glory be to the Father and to the Son and to the Holy Ghost:

℟: As it was in the beginning, is now, and ever shall be, world without end. Amen.

℣: O God, according to Thy name, so is Thy praise unto the end of the earth.

℟: Thy right hand is full of righteousness.

The candidate(s) shall come to the chancel rail, and the pastor, turning to her (them), shall say:

Do you desire admission into the altar guild of _____?

Candidate(s): I do.

Pastor: Do you promise to conform to the rules of the altar guild as long as you are a member of it?

Candidate(s): I do.

Pastor: Do you promise to do the work of the altar guild reverently?

Candidate(s): I do.

Pastor: Do you promise to do your work faithfully and regularly?

Candidate(s): I do.

Pastor: I admit you into membership in the altar guild of ⸺⸺⸺ ⸺⸺⸺ in the name of the Father and of the Son ✠ and of the Holy Ghost. Depart in peace.

The new member(s) shall return to the pew, and all shall kneel.

The Kyrie

The Lord's Prayer

℣: The Lord be with you.

℟: And with thy spirit.

Pastor: Let us pray. Heavenly Father, who hast called this Thy servant (these Thy servants) to a special service in Thy church, teach her (them) the work of the altar guild, help her (them) to fulfill it always with reverence and devotion, and bestow upon her (them) Thy grace and blessings; through Jesus Christ, Thy Son, our Lord, who liveth and reigneth with Thee and the Holy Ghost, ever one God, world without end.

℟: Amen.

All shall rise.

Pastor: The grace of our Lord Jesus Christ ✠ and the love of God and the communion of the Holy Ghost be with you all.

℟: Amen.

✠   ✠   ✠

RUBRIC: This office may be used within the order of service for Matins or Vespers. If so, it shall be inserted after the Canticle, and only that part shall be used which is spoken at the chancel rail. The Collect, however, shall be included among the petitions in the Prayers section of the order of service.

CHAPTER IV

About Devotions and Programs
for Altar Guild Meetings

Devotions

If possible, morning altar guild meetings should begin in church with the Order of Matins, and afternoon or evening meetings with the Order of Vespers. From the church the altar guild should then go to its regular meeting place. At the end of the meeting the pastor or, in his absence, the altar guild director may close with one of the suitable collects printed below.

Should it be impossible to begin the meeting with Matins or Vespers in church, the meeting may be opened in the regular meeting place with the following devotion.

✠ ✠ ✠

A hymn may be sung.

℣: Make haste, O God, to deliver me:

℟: Make haste to help me, O Lord.

All: Glory be to the Father and to the Son and to the Holy Ghost; as it was in the beginning, is now, and ever shall be, world without end. Amen.

Psalm 1, 15, 101, or 112 may then be said. The following Antiphon may be spoken before the Psalm and after the Gloria Patri of the Psalm.

You who fear the Lord, trust in the Lord! He is their Help and their Shield. (Ps. 115:11)

The Collect

A suitable collect from those given below may then be said.

The Meeting

At the end of the meeting, another suitable collect from those given below may be said, or all may say the Lord's Prayer.

✠ ✠ ✠

COLLECTS AND PRAYERS

Before a Meeting

Direct us, O Lord, in all our doings with Thy most gracious favor, and further us with Thy continual help, that in all our works begun, continued, and ended in Thee we may glorify Thy holy name and finally by Thy mercy obtain everlasting life; through Jesus Christ, Thy Son, our Lord, who liveth and reigneth with Thee and the Holy Ghost, ever one God, world without end.

℟: Amen.

✠

Grant, we beseech Thee, merciful Lord, to Thy faithful people pardon and peace, that they may be cleansed from all their sins and serve Thee with a quiet mind; through Jesus Christ, Thy Son, our Lord, who liveth and reigneth with Thee and the Holy Ghost, ever one God, world without end.

℟: Amen.

✠

Almighty God, grant, we beseech Thee, that we may handle holy things with reverence and perform our work with such faithfulness and devotion that it may be acceptable to Thee and obtain Thy blessings; through Jesus Christ, Thy Son, our Lord, who liveth and reigneth with Thee and the Holy Ghost, ever one God, world without end.

℟: Amen.

✠

Blessed Lord Jesus, who didst love Thy Father's house, help us to love Thy service and Thy church, that as Solomon was taught to build and adorn the temple, so we, to whom has been committed here the care of Thy altar and sanctuary, may perform our holy work with pure hearts and hands; who livest and reignest with the Father and the Holy Ghost, ever one God, world without end.

℟: Amen.

After a Meeting

Grant us, we beseech Thee, almighty God, a steadfast faith in Jesus Christ, a cheerful hope in Thy mercy, and a sincere love to Thee and to all our fellowmen; through the same Jesus Christ, Thy Son, our Lord, who liveth and reigneth with Thee and the Holy Ghost, ever one God, world without end.

℟: Amen.

✠

O God, who through the grace of Thy Holy Spirit dost pour the gifts of love into the hearts of Thy faithful people, grant unto Thy servants health, both of mind and of body, that they may love Thee with their whole strength and with their whole heart perform those things which are pleasing unto Thee; through Jesus Christ, Thy Son, our Lord, who liveth and reigneth with Thee and the same Holy Spirit, ever one God, world without end.

℟: Amen.

✠

Almighty God, who hast given Thine only Son to be unto us both a sacrifice for sin and also an example of godly life, give us grace that we may always most thankfully receive this, His inestimable benefit, and also daily endeavor ourselves to follow the blessed steps of His most holy life; through the same Jesus Christ, Thy Son, our Lord, who liveth and reigneth with Thee and the Holy Ghost, ever one God, world without end.

℟: Amen.

✠

To God the Father, who loved us and made us acceptable in the Beloved; to God the Son, who loved us and loosed us from our sins by His own blood; to God the Holy Ghost, who sheddeth the love of God abroad in our hearts: to the one true God be all love and all glory for time and for eternity.

℟: Amen.

✠

Now unto Him that is able to keep us from falling and to present us faultless before the presence of His glory with exceeding joy: to the only wise God, our Savior, be glory and majesty, dominion and power, both now and ever.

℟: Amen.

Private Prayers Before and After Work

In the name of the Father and of the Son ✠ and of the Holy Ghost.

Who shall ascend into the hill of the Lord? Or who shall stand in His holy place? He that hath clean hands and a pure heart. (Ps. 24:3, 4)

Almighty God, unto whom all hearts are open, all desires known, and from whom no secrets are hid, cleanse the thoughts of our hearts by the inspiration of the Holy Spirit, that we may perfectly love Thee and worthily magnify Thy holy name; through Jesus Christ, Thy Son, our Lord, who liveth and reigneth with Thee and the Holy Ghost, ever one God, world without end. Amen.

✠

Them hath He filled with wisdom of heart, to work all manner of work, of the engraver and of the cunning workman, and of the embroiderer in blue and in purple, in scarlet and in fine linen, and of the weaver, even of them that do any work and of those that devise cunning work. (Ex. 35:35)

O Lord Jesus Christ, who didst accept the ministry of faithful women during Thy earthly life, accept and bless the work of my hands in the care of the sanctuary, granting me a spirit of reverence for Thy house and worship, and preserving my soul and body as a living temple of Thy presence; to whom with the Father and the Holy Spirit be all honor and glory, now and forever. Amen.

✠

Whatsoever things are true, whatsoever things are honest, whatsoever things are just, whatsoever things are pure, whatsoever things are lovely, whatsoever things are of good report, if there be any virtue and if there be any praise, think on these things. (Phil. 4:8)

Grant me, I beseech Thee, almighty and most merciful God, fervently to desire all things that are pleasing to Thee; and in everything Thou requirest me to do, grant me the knowledge, the will, and the ability to do it as I ought, to the glory of Thy name; through Jesus Christ, Thy Son, our Lord, who liveth and reigneth with Thee and the Holy Ghost, ever one God, world without end. Amen.

✠

Almighty God, grant that I may handle holy things with reverence and that I may perform my work with such faithfulness and devotion that it may be acceptable to Thee and receive Thy blessings; through Jesus Christ, Thy Son, our Lord. Amen.

✠

O God, accept and bless the work of my hands and all who minister to Thee in the care and adornment of Thy sanctuary, that Thy holy name may be glorified; through Jesus Christ, Thy Son, our Lord. Amen.

✠

O Lord, our God, quicken my heart.
> Let me serve Thee in all humility,
> Let me serve Thee in all reverence,
> Let me serve Thee in all obedience.
>> Give me a clean heart,
>> Give me clean hands,
>> Give me clean thoughts.

Through Jesus Christ, our Lord. Amen.

Programs

Setting up the programs for the altar guild meetings is primarily the concern of the pastor and the altar guild director. They will provide good programs: programs which give the members something to learn and something to do. Furthermore, the program will constantly emphasize that what the guild learns and does is not an end in itself but an aid to the church's worship.

Altar Guild Manuals

A book such as this one will provide programs for many, many meetings. Every member can be provided a copy, and at every meeting a part of it can be studied and discussed chapter by chapter. In most cases what has been learned can then be practiced in the same meeting.

The subjects given in the manuals can also be supplemented with information from other books. For example, the subject of clerical vestments can be expanded by making a study of the historical development of the vestments and modern ideas about their design, shape, and ornamentation.

Practical Demonstrations

From time to time the guild should meet in the chancel for practical demonstrations of what has to be done before and after church services. Actually seeing things done is especially important for new members, but it will also be helpful as a refresher for the older members.

Visual Aids

In line with such demonstrations is the use of visual aids. Slides and filmstrips are available on such subjects as church buildings, the preparation of the altar, clerical vestments, Christian symbols, and the Communion service.

The filmstrip "Duties of the Altar Guild" is a three-part filmstrip dealing with (I) Paraments and vestments, (II) Communion vessels and linens, and (III) Functions and duties of the Altar Guild, which has been prepared as a companion piece to this manual.

The Covenant Altar Guild of the Lutheran Church of the Covenant, 19000 Libby Rd., Maple Heights 39, Ohio, has prepared a set of colored slides on "Altar Preparations." A filmstrip on "Our Lutheran Symbols," by Frederick Rest, is available from the United Church Press, 1505 Race St., Philadelphia 2, Pa. Two filmstrips produced by Luthercraft Productions, "The Order of the Holy Communion" and "The Lutheran Liturgy," may be obtained from *Response*, 2375 Como Ave., St. Paul 8, Minn. Morehouse-Barlow Co., Inc., New York, Chicago, or San Francisco, has slides on "The Vestments of the Church," "The Sacred Vessels," "Care of the Sanctuary," "Eucharistic Appointments," and "The House of God." [1]

Other Program Subjects

In addition to the subjects discussed in this book, the following are especially suitable for altar guild programs: [2]

The rite and ceremonies of the Holy Communion service

The rite and ceremonies of Holy Baptism

The rite and ceremonies of the confirmation service

The rite and ceremonies of the wedding service

The rite and ceremonies of Christian funeral services

The rite and ceremonies of matins

The rite and ceremonies of vespers

[1] For further information on filmstrips and slides, you may wish to consult the current *Guide to Audiovisual Materials* of the Audiovisual Aids Service of Concordia Publishing House, 3558 S. Jefferson Ave., St. Louis, Mo. 63118, or write to *Una Sancta*, 195 Maujer St., Brooklyn, N. Y. 11206, or Fortress Press, 2900 Queen Lane, Philadelphia, Pa. 19129.

[2] For study aids on each topic, see Chap. VI, pp. 33—37.

The function of acolytes, or altar boys

Lutheran worship in the 16th and 17th centuries

The history of the decline of Lutheran liturgical worship

The history of Lutheran worship in the U. S. A.

The church's worship in the Old Testament Scriptures

The church's worship in the New Testament Scriptures

The church's worship in the first five centuries after Christ

Christian customs in observance of Advent

Christian customs in observance of Christmas and Epiphany

Christian customs in observance of Lent

Christian customs in observance of Eastertide

The history of the church year

Living in Christ through the church year

Demonstration of stitches in needlework

Demonstration of sewing the sacred linens

Demonstration of sewing paraments

Demonstration of sewing the vestments

Demonstration of embroidering linens and paraments

Demonstration of church flower arrangement

CHAPTER V

About the Devotional Life of the Altar Guild Member

"It is most important," writes G. Martin Ruoss in his *Altar Guild Workbook*, "that Guild members maintain an active personal devotional life." [1]

To this all altar guild members will agree. But how are they going to carry out such a devotional life?

First of all, altar guild members carry it out by establishing for themselves definite times, places, and forms of prayer and by disciplining themselves to observe these times, places, and forms as regularly as possible. By times of prayer we mean Sundays, feast days, and specific hours of each day. Places of prayer are the church building and a certain location in the home, perhaps a bedroom furnished with a crucifix and *prie-dieu*, or prayer desk. The forms of prayer we shall discuss later. All these things are important. In the other affairs of life we observe order and self-discipline. We go to bed and rise at more or less fixed times, eat our meals at regular hours, and follow a planned schedule every day, week, month, and year. Our devotional life should be ordered and disciplined in much the same way.

Second, the devotional life of the altar guild members is carried out in the framework and spirit of the liturgy. The Lutheran Church is a liturgical church. This means that it has retained the liturgy. The liturgy is properly the Holy Communion service, of which the sermon is but one part. But the term liturgy includes also all other worship services of the universal church, as well as the traditional rites (orders of service), ceremonies (actions, music, symbols, church year), and physical properties (building, altar, vessels, vestments) used in the observance of these services. These rites, ceremonies, and physical properties are not in themselves worship, but they are the inevitable companions of worship.

All churches have rites and ceremonies of some kind. These are liturgical if they are expressive of the worship of the universal church. They are unliturgical if they express no more than personal or group devotion. The rites and ceremonies of the Lutheran Church are liturgical. They are evidences of her link with the past, especially with the Western branch of the universal Christian church. They are a rich and precious heritage. To appreciate this heritage, the church must constantly interpret it to her members, defend it, use it, and cultivate it reverently.

[1] Rev. ed. (Philadelphia: Muhlenberg Press, 1955), p. 9.

The center of the church's liturgy is the Holy Communion service.[2] In obedience to our Lord's command, "This do in remembrance of Me," and the example of the early church, "they continued steadfastly in the apostles' doctrine and fellowship and in the breaking of bread [the Holy Communion service] and in prayers," the Lutheran Church regards the Holy Communion service, or the Mass, as the chief service. In our Lutheran Confessions we read: ". . . one common Mass is observed among us on every holy day, and on other days, if any desire the sacrament, it is also administered to those who ask for it." [3] "Every Lord's Day many in our circles use the Lord's Supper, but only after they have been instructed, examined, and absolved." [4] "In our churches Mass is celebrated every Sunday and on other festivals. . . ." [5]

Also our daily prayers should be liturgical. According to the service book, the official daily prayers of the church are matins and vespers.[6] They and the Holy Communion service belong together. One can compare them to the sun and its planets; the Holy Communion service is the sun around which the church's daily prayers revolve. Matins and vespers prepare for the Holy Communion service, and they also carry the blessing of the Communion service into the other days of the week. The Communion service does not begin with the Introit, nor does it end with the Benediction. It begins with the first vespers of the evening before and continues in matins and vespers to sanctify the ferial days following the Sunday or feast day.

Matins and vespers have two purposes: (1) to serve as the daily, objective prayers of the church and (2) to help the individual member grow up in Christ. He who prays matins and vespers feels himself united with the whole church. He is not just an individual in dialog with God. This is not private prayer. In private prayer the individual is the only one praying. Being what he is, he thinks mainly of himself and the persons and things that concern him. It is therefore more or less individualistic exercise. But in liturgical prayer the individual is not the only one who prays. The church prays. The individual is a member of the communion of saints, a leaf on the tree, a partaker of the life and activity of the church — a branch sapping nourishment from the Vine. All the feelings, thoughts, and experiences of the church are reechoed in his prayers even

2 *The Lutheran Hymnal* (St. Louis: Concordia Publishing House, 1941), pp. 15—31 and the rubrics and propers on pp. 3, 4, 53—94, 102—119, 159—161, 168—851; *Service Book and Hymnal of the Lutheran Church in America*, Music Ed. (Minneapolis, Minn.: Augsburg Publishing House et al., 1958), pp. 1—14 and the other rubrics and propers on pp. 15—128, 156—241, 274—279, and the hymnal section.

3 Augsburg Confession XXIV 34 (from Latin text); *The Book of Concord: The Confessions of the Evangelical Lutheran Church*, trans. and ed. Theodore G. Tappert in collaboration with Jaroslav Pelikan, Robert H. Fischer, Arthur C. Piepkorn (Philadelphia: Muhlenberg Press, 1959), p. 60.

4 Apology XV 40; ibid., p. 220.

5 Apology XXIV 1; ibid., p. 249.

6 *The Lutheran Hymnal*, pp. 32—45 and the rubrics and propers on pp. 3, 4, 53, 95—851; *Service Book and Hymnal*, pp. 129—148 and the rubrics and propers on pp. 149—237, 274—285, and the hymnal section.

as they were in the lauds and the laments of the psalmists. Thus he is raised above his little self. The church is praying, and he is praying in and with the church.

But in praying matins and vespers the individual does not lose his identity. In nature an individual tree does not lose its identity as the seasons shift to give it growth, flowers, and fruit and then strip it bare of foliage and all. So in liturgical prayer the Word commemorated in the church year gives the individual growth in Christ. It helps him bear the fruits of faith and brings peace, comfort, and protection to him in the conflicts of life.

Let us now point out a few things that may be helpful in praying matins and vespers daily.

1. In private recitation these offices are prayed straight through and with greater freedom than in public recitation. But we shall do well to observe all the rubrics and ceremonies according to our circumstances.

2. We say both the versicles and the responses when we say the office alone; the Salutation and the Benediction are omitted.

3. In silent recitation it is good to move the lips in token that we are saying these offices in union and communion with the church.

4. Before we begin, we may bless ourselves with the sign of the cross and say: "In the name of the Father and of the Son and of the Holy Ghost. Amen. O Lord, open Thou my lips that I may praise Thy holy name; cleanse my heart from all vain, perverse, and wandering thoughts; enlighten my mind and inflame my heart so that I may pray this office reverently, devoutly, and attentively and that I may be heard in the presence of Thy divine Majesty; through Jesus Christ, Thy Son, our Lord, who liveth and reigneth with Thee and the Holy Ghost, ever one God, world without end. Amen."

5. At "O Lord, open Thou my lips" we may trace a small sign of the cross on our lips, and at the next versicle, "Make haste . . ." we may make the full sign. Then we may bow profoundly while saying: "Glory be to the Father. . . ."

6. From Septuagesima to Holy Saturday, instead of the Alleluia we may say: "Praise be to Thee, O Lord, King of eternal glory."

7. We use the propers for the season as found in *The Lutheran Hymnal*, pp. 95—99; for example, the Invitatory.

8. In the Venite we may bow deeply or kneel when we say: "Oh, come, let us worship and bow down; let us kneel before the Lord, our Maker."

9. We repeat the Invitatory as an antiphon after the Venite.

10. The Lutheran Liturgy edition of the Lutheran Church Calendar, published by the Ashby Company of Erie, Pa., gives suggestions for proper office hymns.

11. Psalms appointed for Sundays and feasts are given in *The Lutheran Hymnal*, pp. 159, 160, 164—166. On other days, Psalms 1—109 are prayed in matins and Psalms 110—150 in vespers. We may pray one of these in each office, beginning with the first vespers of Advent, and when we come to the end, we start again with Psalm 1 in matins and Psalm 110 in vespers. The longer psalms may be divided: *Psalm 18*:1-24, 25-50; *37*:1-22, 23-40; *78*:1-16, 17-39, 40-72; *89*:1-18, 19-37, 38-52; *104*:1-12, 13-23, 24-35; *105*:1-15, 16-27, 28-45; *106*:1-31, 32-48; *107*:1-22, 23-43; *109*:1-20, 21-31; *118*:1-13, 14-29; *119*, two parts each time; *136*:1-9, 10-26; *139*:1-12, 13-24; *147*:1-11, 12-20. Psalm 95, the Venite, is omitted. It will be helpful for praying the psalms more meaningfully to remember who speaks in them. Usually it is Christ, Christ and His church, or Christ and His church and the individual member of the church. Sometimes God the Father speaks to Christ or to the individual member in the body of Christ.

12. The lessons for Sundays and feasts are given in *The Lutheran Hymnal*, pp. 159—161. (Note both the first and the second series of Epistles and Gospels.) On other days follow the schedule on pp. 161—164. By following these schedules we read nearly the whole Bible devotionally each year. This is an objective of liturgical prayer. It wants to lead all Christians through the whole of Scripture at least once a year.

13. The matin Canticle for Sundays and feasts is the Te Deum Laudamus, except in penitential seasons, and for other days it is the Benedictus. The Canticle for early vespers is the Magnificat and for late vespers or compline the Nunc Dimittis. The Canticle is the high point of the office, for it praises God for Christ and His redemptive work. Part of the Sunday or feast-day Gospel is said as an antiphon before and after the Canticle, except for the Te Deum. For a change the other canticles on pp. 120—122 may be used: in matins on feasts and during Eastertide the Benedicite Omnia Opera; in Eastertide and Ascensiontide the Dignus Est Agnus; on any Monday the Confitebor Tibi; on Tuesday the Ego Dixi; Wednesday the Exultavit Cor Meum; Thursday the Cantemus Domino; Friday the Domine, Audivi; and Saturday the Audite, Coeli. In vespers the Dignus Est Agnus is proper during Eastertide, Ascensiontide, and the Trinity season.

14. In the concluding prayer section, one of the collects after the Sunday or feast-day collect should be a collect of intercession. One plan is this, that on Mondays we may pray for workers or special undertakings or our family or friends; on Tuesdays (the day Christ disputed the last time with His enemies) for our enemies, schismatics, and the heathen; on Wednesdays (the day Judas bargained to betray our Lord) for sinners and all who neglect to worship and serve Christ; on Thursdays (the day of our Lord's institution of Holy Communion) for the church, its missions,

officers, pastors, teachers, schools, and seminaries; on Fridays (the day of Christ's crucifixion) for sufferers, the sick, the persecuted, and the dying; and on Saturdays for our country, nations, rulers, and world peace.

The altar guild member may also wish to use other forms of prayer and devotion. Here the field is wide open, ranging all the way from materials of a liturgical character and in harmony with the liturgy to forms of prayer which are nonliturgical and aliturgical. However, once a person lives the liturgical life, he soon learns to distinguish between the good and the bad.

It should also be said that liturgical and fixed prayers are to lead an individual to *ex corde* or extemporaneous prayer in his private devotions. When a person has prayed the church's prayers, he should pour out his heart to God in his own way and words. Such free praying belongs to a liturgical devotional life. The prayers of the church will stimulate it. Therefore it is a good rule to start with the church's prayers, to pray psalms and other fixed prayers, and then to close the books and simply speak to God.

In the *Service Book and Hymnal* the psalms appointed for Sundays and feasts are given on pp. 282–283, and the lessons for matins and vespers on Sundays and holy days on pp. 280–281. This book does not contain a schedule of weekday lessons.

The Daily Office, edited by Herbert Lindemann (St. Louis: Concordia Publishing House, 1965), gives the propers for daily matins and vespers and for all minor festivals of the church year. The traditional "little hours" of prayer are also included in an appendix.

CHAPTER VI

About Church Services and Rubrics

All the rites and rubrics for Lutheran church worship are given in the Lutheran service books. But since the altar guild exists for the very purpose of helping the church to observe these services more reverently, devoutly, and beautifully, through more intensive private and group study the members of the altar guild should grow in their understanding and appreciation of them. Members should learn something about the services' history and meaning and the way they are properly and traditionally conducted. Detailed background information about the services obviously cannot be included in an altar guild guide. However, a variety of excellent books and other resources for further study is readily available.[1] We have listed some of these sources in the chapter "Helpful Books, Magazines, and Visual Aids" (pp. 126—128). Perhaps the congregation can be encouraged to include some of these items in its church library so members of the altar guild may conveniently consult them.

CHURCH SERVICES
The Chief Service

The chief service of the church was instituted by our Lord on the night in which He was betrayed. In obedience to His command, "This do in remembrance of Me," the church has "done" this service down through the centuries. It has been called the Breaking of Bread, the Lord's Supper, the Holy Eucharist, the Mass, the Sacrament of the Altar, and the Holy Communion service. As the chief service, it is and ought to be central in the church's worship; the other services revolve around it like the planets around the sun. Most of the other services are also derived from it, being built on one or the other of its component parts.

Communion of the sick is an extension of the Holy Communion service from the church to those who are unable to attend. Holy Communion is true to its name, for it is truly a "communion" in which the many are one body as they partake of the one bread and one cup (1 Cor. 10:16, 17). It is for the sake of symbolizing this communion that the Lutheran Church retains the common cup, the chalice. The chalice is the preferred choice of the Lutheran Church, for without exception the Word of God speaks of the cup in the singular in Holy Communion contexts. In the Words

[1] For very brief discussion of the meaning and traditions of Lutheran worship, see Paul H. D. Lang, *The Lutheran Order of Services* (St. Louis: Concordia Publishing House, 1952); the tract "Lutheran Church Worship" (New York: American Lutheran Publicity Bureau, 1953); and the tract "Questions Often Asked by a Newcomer into a Lutheran Church" (Ridgefield Park, N. J.: Una Sancta Press, 1954).

of Institution, Christ says that all should drink of the one cup, and we are told that they all drank of the one cup. This cup is called the cup of the Lord.[2]

The Holy Baptism Service

Holy Baptism was also instituted by Christ Himself. It is the sacrament of initiation into the Christian life and of membership in the church. It therefore leads into the chief service, the Holy Communion service, the purpose of which is to preserve and increase the new life in Christ, stimulate its growth, and bring it to perfection. Since Holy Baptism incorporates into the body of Christ, the church, the baptismal service is logically and usually carried out in connection with one of the other church services so that the congregation is present and participates actively in its performance. The rubrics of *The Lutheran Liturgy* direct: "Unless otherwise ordered in a Congregation, public Baptism may be administered after the Opening Hymn, in which case the Opening Hymn may well be a baptismal hymn." [3]

The Confession and Absolution Service

The service of confession and absolution is based on Christ's words: "Whosoever sins ye remit, they are remitted unto them; and whosoever sins ye retain, they are retained" (John 20:23). Confession and absolution is a continuation of Holy Baptism. ". . . Baptism, both by its power and by its signification, comprehends also the third sacrament, formerly called Penance, which is really nothing else than Baptism. . . . If you live in repentance, therefore, you are walking in Baptism, which not only announces this new life but also produces, begins, and promotes it. . . . Repentance, therefore, is nothing else than a return and approach to Baptism, to resume and practice what had earlier been begun but abandoned." [4] The Lutheran Church has retained the practice of private confession and absolution, but it has also introduced a general confession, either as a separate service or as part of one of the other church services.

The Confirmation Service

Confirmation with the laying on of hands is connected with the baptism of infants, because baptized infants need to be instructed and confirmed when they reach the age of reason. Instruction in the Christian faith precedes adult baptism; in infant baptism the instruction follows Holy Baptism. Confirmation, however, is in no sense a graduation from school. For that reason a commercial confirmation gown which resembles the graduation gowns used in high schools and colleges is unsuitable. Confirmation is the beginning of communicant membership with its privileges, duties, and blessings. Among these duties is the continuation of Christian

[2] See the question on the chalice in Paul H. D. Lang, *Questions Often Asked by a Newcomer into a Lutheran Church* (Brooklyn: Una Sancta Press, 1952), pp. 8 f.

[3] (St. Louis: Concordia Publishing House, 1955 or later printing), p. 419.

[4] Large Catechism IV 74, 75, 79; *The Book of Concord: The Confessions of the Evangelical Lutheran Church*, trans. and ed. Theodore G. Tappert in collaboration with Jaroslav Pelikan, Robert H. Fischer, Arthur C. Piepkorn (Philadelphia: Muhlenberg Press, 1959), pp. 445, 446. See also Augsburg Confession XXV; ibid., pp. 61—63.

education. What the traditional dress for confirmation children is, we shall discuss in a later chapter. Like the Holy Baptism service, confirmation should be included in a church service in which the congregation is present.

The Morning Service Without Communion

The morning service without Communion, also sometimes called the ante-Communion, is simply the first part of the chief service, the Holy Communion service, used as a separate service. For its conclusion an offertory, general prayer, and benediction are added after the sermon.

The Matin and Vesper Services

Matins and vespers are the daily prayers of the church which continue the chief service of Sundays and feasts through the weekdays following them. The Lutheran Church contemplated their daily use even if only a very few people could attend them. It should be noted that the Canticle, the Nunc Dimittis, is the traditional compline Canticle. It is not proper in an early vespers, but only in a very late vesper or bedtime service.

The Marriage Service

A wedding in church is a church service as solemn and reverent as any other church service. It is not held to glorify man but to ask and receive the blessings of God on a special ordinance which He Himself ordained. Church worship standards apply to the whole wedding, including the music. Sometimes a marriage is solemnized along with the celebration of Holy Communion. Such a combined service is called a nuptial Eucharist. The Holy Communion service adds to the solemnity and joy of the wedding and expresses the communion with Christ and with the members of the congregation of those who are being united in Christ in holy matrimony. Therefore a nuptial Eucharist may be permitted only if both bride and groom are communicant members and if it is understood that all communicant members who are present and desire the sacrament may partake of it.

The Ordination Service

The rite of ordination is the service in which the church formally admits a man to the public ministry and confers heavenly gifts on him by the laying on of hands (2 Tim. 1:6-14). According to ancient and good tradition, the rite of ordination is properly incorporated in a Holy Communion service.

The Service for the Burial of the Dead

According to the Lutheran rite, the service for the burial of the dead is divided into three parts. Each part is held in a different place: at the house or funeral home, in the church, and at the grave. It envisions the participation of the congregation and all the standards in music and ceremonies of a church worship service.

Other Services and Blessings

Lutheran service books provide rites for many other services, such as installations of pastors, professors, teachers, and members of church councils; cornerstone layings for church buildings; dedications of parish houses; consecrations of deacons in commissioning foreign missionaries; churchings of women after childbirth; and receptions of new members. Rites for the blessing of objects are also provided; for example, the blessing of church sites, cemeteries, sacred vessels and furnishings, windows, bells, organs, homes, and the like. The altar guild would do well to become acquainted with all these offices.[5]

Rubrics

A rubric is a suggestion, direction, or rule as to how the services of the church are to be carried out and their parts properly performed. The name comes from a Latin word meaning red. The service directions are called rubrics because they were once written in red ink, while the wording of the rite itself was written in black ink.

Since church services are "done," i. e., involve action, the development of ceremony in the doing is inevitable. But if left unregulated, the ceremony might come to overshadow the substance and primary purpose of the service. Therefore the church wisely prescribes and makes suggestions for the proper ordering and directing of its worship services. This it does through the rubrics.

Shall, May, and Should Rubrics

When the word *shall* is used in the rubrics, the rule has binding force and is obligatory. For example, "The Congregation shall rise, and the Minister, facing the altar, shall say."

The verb *may* allows a choice and leaves the matter optional. For example, "The sign of the cross may be made at the Trinitarian Invocation and at the words of the Nicene Creed, 'And the life of the world to come.'"

A *should* rubric indicates preferred action. "The Introit for the day, including the Gloria Patri, should either be sung or spoken throughout" means that if a choice is to be made between singing or speaking the Gloria Patri when the rest of the Introit is spoken, the better choice is to speak the Gloria Patri. Here is a should rubric concerning color use: "In some parts of the Lutheran Church green is used from Septuagesima through Shrove Tuesday. In that case white should be used from Matins on January 14 until, but not at, Vespers on the Saturday before Septuagesima." Sometimes the word *preferable* is used instead of shall, as in the rubric, "Since the Preparation is not a part of the Service proper, it is preferable that the Officiant and the Congregation speak the entire Preparatory Service."

General Rubrics

Directions which are not limited to a specific item of a worship service or office are called general rubrics. They regulate the discharge of the church year, the use of paraments, and many other devotional details. The following is a general rubric on sacramental linens: "When not in use

[5] For the Lutheran rites and rubrics for all these services, see *The Lutheran Liturgy* and *The Lutheran Agenda* (St. Louis: Concordia Publishing House).

on the altar, the sacramental linens should be properly folded and kept in the *Burse,* a square envelope made of strong cardboard, covered with silk or heavy linen."

Particular Rubrics

Directives for specific details of the rites and ceremonies are called particular rubrics. These rubrics are not collected and arranged separately, as general rubrics usually are, but accompany the rites themselves. For example, "Then shall follow the General Prayer" is a particular rubric.

Learn to Know the Rubrics

Many of the rubrics also govern the work and establish specific duties for the altar guild. Among such rubrics are those which pertain to the meaning and use of liturgical colors, the sacred linens and vessels, the paraments and vestments. These rubrics the altar guild must certainly know. However, the interest of the altar guild is not limited to the use of colors, linens, and vestments. The guild is concerned about the church's worship as a whole, especially the ceremonies or externals of this worship. Therefore guild members should devote time to the study of the rubrics, both general and particular, so that they may become familiar with all of them.

For further information on the rites and ceremonies of the Lutheran Church's worship services, see Paul H. D. Lang, *Ceremony and Celebration* (St. Louis: Concordia Publishing House, 1965), an evangelical guide for Christian practice in corporate worship.

CHAPTER VII

About Liturgical Terms

The members of the altar guild should learn — at least to the extent necessary for their work — the technical terms which are reverently used when we speak of the house of God and of the things employed in the church's worship. We call the entrance hall of a church building not a vestibule but the narthex. The place where the people gather for worship in the church is called not an auditorium but the nave. Such technical terms have come down to us through long and unbroken usage in the Christian church and serve to distinguish the sacred from the secular. It is more reverent and more edifying, hence more appropriate, to call the container in which water is brought to the baptismal font an ewer than to refer to it as a pitcher. As we proceed in our discussion, we shall call each object utilized in worship by its ecclesiastical name so that all who serve at the Lord's altar may become familiar with technical ecclesiastical language. We offer here a selective glossary of such terms.

Glossary

Absolution. The declaration of the forgiveness of sins. In the office of confession and absolution, it is the divinely authorized declaration pronounced by the confessor (pastor) on the confessing penitent.

Acolyte. An assistant to the minister in the public services, one of whose duties it is to light and to extinguish the altar candles. Usually a young man or boy; sometimes called an altar boy. The acolyte is vested in cassock and cotta (or surplice); in some churches he wears an alb.

Agenda. One of the names given books containing the orders or rites of the divine services, primarily intended for the use of the clergy. To be distinguished from the general meaning "order of business" for a meeting.

Agnus Dei. Latin for "Lamb of God." A liturgical hymn based on the words of John the Baptist about our Lord in John 1:29 and sung during the distribution of the Sacrament of the Altar and after the Litany.

Alb. A long white linen vestment properly worn at the celebration of Holy Communion and usually worn over a cassock. See chapter on vestments, p. 89.

Alleluia. The anglicized and preferred form of *hallelujah,* Hebrew for "praise ye the Lord." A Scriptural ejaculation or ascription of joy and praise variously used in the church's liturgy.

Alms bag. A container for gathering the offerings in church. See p. 78.

Altar. The most important article of church furnishing and the focal point of divine worship. See chapter on the altar, p. 51.

Amice. A linen clerical vestment worn about the neck and shoulders over a cassock and under an alb. See chapter on vestments, p. 89.

Ante-Communion. The first part of the Holy Communion service, sometimes called the Mass of the catechumens or the ministry of the Word. Includes all that precedes the Preface of the Communion office. Ante-Communion is also used to designate the common service without the celebration of Communion, the preaching service.

Antependium. An ornamental parament suspended before the altar, pulpit, or lectern.

Antiphon. A psalm verse or brief Scripture text said before and after the psalms or portions of the psalms and before and after most canticles.

Apse. In a basilica the semicircular space at the end of the nave. In a Gothic church the semicircular or polygonal end of the chancel or the end of an aisle or transept. See p. 49.

Benedicite Omnia Opera. Latin for "all works, praise ye." A canticle in praise of God by all nature. Also called the Song of the Three Children; cf. vv. 35-65 of the apocryphal book of the same name. In *The Lutheran Hymnal,* p. 120; *The Lutheran Liturgy,* pp. 282, 283.

Benedictus. Latin for "blessed." One of the canticles at matins. The song of Zacharias from Luke 1:68-79.

Benedictus Qui Venit. Latin for "blessed who cometh." The last verse of the Sanctus in the Holy Communion service; based on Matt. 21:9.

Bidding Prayer. A special form of liturgical prayer consisting of a series of petitions, each of which includes an invitation to pray for a special object while standing, silence for private prayer while kneeling, a collect spoken by the minister in summary of the congregation's prayers, and a concluding Amen by the people. See such a prayer specially appointed for Good Friday, *The Lutheran Liturgy,* pp. 274—277.

Bowing. An external act or ceremony of reverence and respect. In church services we may bow toward the altar during the Gloria Patri, when the holy name Jesus is spoken (Phil. 2:9-11), at the words "And was made man" in the Nicene Creed, and at other times.

Breviary. The book(s) for praying the Divine Office, or canonical hours. *See also* Canonical hours.

Burse. A container like an envelope for storing the corporal, purificators, and other linens and for carrying them to and from the altar for the Holy Communion. See chapter on paraments, p. 78.

Canonical hours. The daily prayer services of the church, including traditionally Matins, Lauds, Prime, Terce, Sext, Nones, Vespers, and Compline. Lutheran use preserves matin and vesper services and parts of Lauds, Prime, and Compline.

Canticle. A nonmetrical sacred song chanted or sung in church services, such as the Te Deum and the Magnificat.

Cassock. A long black garment, formfitting from neck to waist, full and flowing below the waist, worn by clergymen and others. See chapter on vestments, p. 85.

Celebrant. In the celebration of the Eucharist, the officiating minister as distinguished from his assistants.

Censer. A vessel in which incense is burned.

Cerecloth. A wax-treated linen cloth placed first over the mensa of the altar and under the other altar cloths. See chapter on altar linens, p. 80.

Ceremonial. The prescribed acts, gestures, and movements accompanying a liturgical rite; or the total actions which accompany the service, including speech, music, and use of objects.

Chalice. The liturgical cup used in the Holy Communion service. See chapter on sacred vessels, p. 65.

Chalice veil. The small cloth with which the Communion chalice is vested, or covered, before and after the consecration and distribution of the elements. See chapter on paraments, p. 77.

Chancel. The east end of a church, above and beyond the nave and beyond the chancel rail.

Chancel rail. The rail separating nave and chancel or choir and sanctuary. At it worshipers usually kneel to receive Holy Communion or for other acts of worship. See p. 59.

Chasuble. The principal liturgical vestment of the celebrant at Holy Communion or on high festivals. See chapter on clerical vestments, p. 90.

Choir. (1) The part of the church, between the nave and the sanctuary, reserved for a group of clerical or liturgical singers. See p. 47. (2) A group of singers who assist musically in church services.

Chrisom. A white cloth, robe, or mantle thrown over a child when baptized; a sign of innocence, the innocence of Christ, appropriated in Holy Baptism. See p. 82.

Ciborium. (1) A vessel used for storing or in distributing Holy Communion wafers. See chapter on sacred vessels, p. 65. (2) A canopy above the altar.

Cincture. A cord or band with which alb and cassock are girded. See chapter on clerical vestments, p. 85.

Compline. The service which completes the day. In Lutheran usage, vespers and the evening suffrages incorporate some features of traditional Compline.

Confiteor. Latin for "I confess." (1) The preparatory confessional part of a regular church service. (2) The confession in a service of confession and absolution. (3) A separate confessional service.

Cope. An ornamented cloak usually made in the liturgical colors and worn over an alb or surplice. See chapter on clerical vestments, p. 92.

Corpus. A carved figure attached to a cross in representation of Christ, emphasizing that Christ became man to be our Redeemer and Lord. See p. 52.

Cotta. A vestment like a surplice but shorter, worn over a cassock by acolytes, choir members, and organists. See p. 92 on acolytes.

Credence. A table or shelf on the south wall of the sanctuary for use in the Communion service. See p. 61.

Crosier. A pastoral staff or crook of a bishop or abbot; still used particularly by bishops in Sweden.

Crucifer. One who carries a processional crucifix or cross.

Cruet. A crystal or glass vessel used as a container for wine or water in the Communion service. See chapter on sacred vessels, p. 65.

Deacon. A clergyman who assists a pastor in the celebration of Holy Communion or in other solemn services.

Dossal or *Dorsal.* A permanent hanging back of and above the altar. See chapter on the altar, pp. 55–57.

Doxology. An ascription of praise to the Triune God.

Elevation. The act of lifting the consecrated Communion elements before the people.

Epistle side. The right, or south, side as you face the altar. See p. 47.

Eucharist. Greek for "thanksgiving." The Holy Communion service, the Holy Eucharist.

Eucharistic prayer. In Lutheran use, a special prayer of thanksgiving in the Holy Communion service. *The Lutheran Hymnal* does not include a eucharistic prayer in the rite; the *Service Book and Hymnal* does, "The Prayer of Thanksgiving" on p. 11.

Exorcism. In Holy Baptism, the ceremonial act of casting out the devil by prayer and the sign of the cross.

Fair linen. The top linen on the altar, symbolizing the winding sheet used in the burial of our Lord's body. See chapter on altar linens, p. 80.

Faithful, the. Christian believers, worshipers in church.

Fall. A name sometimes used for the paraments on altar, pulpit, and lectern.

Flagon. A covered vessel into which wine is poured for use in the Holy Communion service. See chapter on sacred vessels, p. 65.

Frontal. An ornamented hanging or parament covering the entire front of the altar. See chapter on paraments, p. 69.

Genuflection. A bending of the right knee to the floor, but distinguished from kneeling.

Gospel side. The left, or north, side as you face the altar. See p. 47.

Gradine. A step or shelf behind and higher than the altar mensa, on which the crucifix, candlesticks, and flowers may stand.

Gradual. A liturgical chant between the Epistle and the Gospel. If an Old Testament lesson is read before the Epistle, the Gradual follows the Lesson before the Epistle, and the alleluia verse follows the Epistle.

Hosanna. Hebrew for "save now." A Messianic acclamation of joy and praise variously used in the church's liturgy.

Intercession. Prayer in behalf of others.

Introit. The liturgical entrance anthem of the morning service and the Holy Communion service, composed of an antiphon, psalm verse or psalm, Gloria Patri, and antiphon repeated.

Invitatory. An invitation to adoration and praise, such as the seasonal antiphon for the Venite in the matin service. Some speak of both antiphon and the Venite together as the Invitatory.

Invocation. (1) A hymn calling on the Holy Ghost, as suggested in the service books for opening the morning service. (2) The words "In the name of the Father and of the Son and of the Holy Ghost" at the beginning of worship services. (3) The opening petitions of the Litany.

Kyrie Eleison. Greek for "Lord, have mercy." A greeting and supplication. In pre-Christian times the phrase was used in greeting a king when he visited his people.

Lectern. A stand at which the lessons are read in worship services. See p. 59.

Lection. Two or more lessons or readings from Holy Scripture as prescribed for worship services.

Litany. An intercessory, penitential, deeply devotional form of liturgical prayer. See the Litany and litany collects in *The Lutheran Liturgy,* pp. 255—261; in the *Service Book and Hymnal,* pp. 156—161. Some responsive and antiphonal prayers are patterned after the litany form.

Liturgiologist. A specialist in the study of the forms of worship and their practice.

Liturgist. A Christian who participates in doing the church's worship. One who leads liturgical worship is also a liturgist, but it is more specific to call him celebrant when he conducts the Holy Communion service and officiant when he conducts a minor service.

Liturgy. The church's worship of God.

Mass. The Holy Communion service. (See Augsburg Confession XXIV: "Of the Mass.")

Matins. The first of the canonical hours, morning prayer.

Mensa. The top of the altar. See p. 52.

Missal. A book containing the propers and ordinary for the church year and intended for use at the altar.

Missal stand. The desk on which the service book rests on the altar during public worship.

Miter. The liturgical hat of a bishop. See p. 92.

Narthex. The vestibule or entrance hall of a church building. See p. 47.

Nave. The main body of a church, extending from narthex or entrance to chancel; the room for the laity. See p. 47.

Oblation. An offering or sacrifice.

Octave. The first and following seven days for the celebration of a feast.

Offertory. The chant associated with the offering of self, bread, wine, and money in the Holy Communion service; e. g., "Create in me a clean heart, O God. . . ."

Officiant. The conductor or leader of a minor service.

Ordinary. (1) The invariable parts of the liturgy. (2) The bishop or other ruling prelate of a diocese.

Orientation. Construction of a church or chapel on an east-west line with the altar at the east end. From this are derived the technical terms referring to the north, east, south, and west sides or parts of a church building even when not so oriented according to the compass. See p. 45.

Orphrey. An ornamental band or border of a parament or vestment. See chapters on paraments and vestments, pp. 69–79, 85–94.

Pall. A cover for a chalice or a coffin. See chapters on linens and vestments, pp. 79, 81, 83.

Paschal candle. A special candle lighted on Easter Eve and extinguished on the feast of the Ascension. See p. 99.

Paten. A plate for the distribution of the wafers in the Holy Communion service. See chapter on vessels, p. 65.

Pericope. A system of lessons appointed for the Sundays and festivals of the church year.

Preces. Prayers in the form of versicles and responses, such as the suffrages.

Propers. The variable parts of the liturgy.

Purificator. A small napkin used to cleanse the rim of the chalice during the distribution of Holy Communion. See chapter on linens, p. 81.

Pyx. The ciborium, or vessel for the Holy Communion wafers. See p. 65.

Reredos. An architectural ornament of wood or stone erected behind the altar. See chapter on the altar, p. 55.

Riddels. Curtains at both sides of the altar. See chapter on the altar, p. 57.

Rite. (1) A formal religious act; the order or form of a divine service. (2) The whole body of services, liturgical actions, and uses employed in worship by the church.

Rituale. A book containing the rites of minor church services or the rites of occasional services.

Rood screen. An ornamental and symbolical screen supporting a crucifix (rood) and separating the nave and choir. See p. 47.

Rubrics. Directions for the conduct of church services. See chapter on rubrics, p. 36.

Sanctuary. The part of a church where the altar is located. See p. 47.

Sanctuary lamp. A constantly burning lamp in the sanctuary. See chapter on the use of lights, p. 98.

Sedilia. Seats in the chancel for clergy. See p. 61.

Server. One who assists an officiating minister.

Sext. The noonday office or service of the church.

Stole. A sacramental clerical vestment as distinguished from a stole of ordinary dress. Worn over an alb or a surplice. See chapter on vestments, p. 90.

Surplice. A white linen vestment falling almost to the ankles, having a round yoke and long wide sleeves. See chapter on vestments, p. 87.

Terce. The morning office or service of the church at about 9:00.

Transept. (1) That part of a cruciform church comparable to the horizontal bar of a cross. (2) In a less strict sense, either end of the crossbar.

Tryptych. A three-paneled ornament behind the altar, the two side panels of which can be folded in to cover the central panel. See p. 57.

Use. The particular body of church ceremonies and customs which prevail in a certain place.

Variables. Parts of the service which change with the Sunday and season; the propers.

Vase. A vessel for flowers to be placed on the gradine of the altar. See p. 110.

Venite. Latin for "come." Psalm 95 sung in matins.

Versicles. Brief responsive verses from the psalms as used in public worship.

Vespers. The early evening office or service of the church.

CHAPTER VIII

About the Church Building

The House of God

The church building is the sacred house of God where Christians assemble in the name of Christ to

1. Celebrate the Holy Communion service, the chief service of the church;

2. Receive God's grace and blessings through His Word and sacraments;

3. Offer God sacrifices of self, prayer, praise, thanksgiving, adoration, and possessions;

4. Edify one another through mutual participation in worship;

5. Engage in the minor services, such as the preaching service, Baptism, confession and absolution, matins, vespers, weddings, and funerals; and

6. Enter at any time for individual prayer and devotions.

Different from Other Buildings

Because of its sacred character and purpose the church building is distinguished from all other buildings and possesses greater dignity.

1. The church is in a unique way the house of God. "How awesome is this place. This is none other than the house of God, and this is the gate of heaven." (Gen. 28:17)

2. The church is the holy place where the "one, holy, Christian (catholic), and apostolic church," the body of Christ, comes to visible expression and is built up. "For we, being many, are one bread and one body, for we are all partakers of that one bread" (1 Cor. 10:17). The church building is therefore a symbol of the body of Christ.

3. The church is the place where heaven is anticipated. Therefore it is a symbol of heaven and the eternal union of God and His people. "Behold, the tabernacle of God is with men." (Rev. 21:3)

Orientation

A church building is properly orientated if its main axis is laid from west to east. Such orientation is a matter of tradition and significant symbolism. The light of God is regarded as rising in the east as does the sun in the natural order. Reference is made to Ezekiel 43:4: "And the glory of the Lord came into the house by the way of the gate whose prospect is toward the east." Since the altar symbolizes the presence of God in the church, it was set in the east end of the building. Thus the

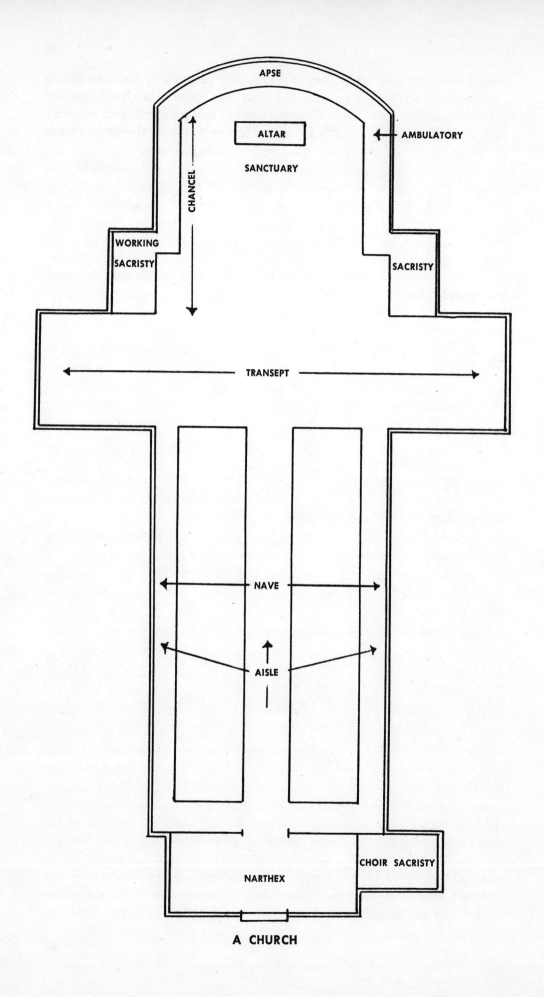

APSE

ALTAR

AMBULATORY

SANCTUARY

CHANCEL

WORKING
SACRISTY

SACRISTY

TRANSEPT

NAVE

AISLE

CHOIR SACRISTY

NARTHEX

A CHURCH

people face the east when they worship, not particularly because facing east is so significant but because the altar, the focus of a church and its worship, is in the east. Even when the ancient custom is followed whereby the celebrant at certain times stands on the east side of the altar, facing the people, both he and the people are turned to the altar.

Not all church buildings are properly or traditionally oriented. It is sometimes impossible or impractical to build a church with the altar in the east. Nor is it absolutely necessary. But proper orientation is taken for granted in church terminology. Regardless of the building's orientation, we speak of the *chancel as in the east,* the *narthex as in the west,* and the *arms of the transept as in the north and south.* We speak of the *east, north, and south walls of the chancel* and of the *north and south horns of the altar.* The *Epistle side is the south side,* and the *Gospel side is the north side.*

Names of the Parts of the Building

A church building has two principal parts, a chancel and a nave. The *chancel* is the room in which the altar is located. The name is derived from a Latin word for a lattice, grating, or screen, for in early Christian times a kind of screen or rail separated the various parts of a basilica, the type of church then used. When such a dividing screen is surmounted by a crucifix (rood), it is called a rood screen.

The *nave* is the main body of the church in which the laity gather. The name comes from the Latin *navis* ("ship"). The church is pictured as a ship sailing the ocean of time, and the body of the church building, its largest room, is thus symbolically called the nave.

In addition to its two principal parts, a church building may have the following parts or rooms:

A *narthex,* a porch, vestibule, or entrance hall attached to the west end of the nave. Usually the main outside door of a church leads into a narthex. Symbolically it is a room providing for a transition from the outside world into the church proper.

The *sanctuary* is the eastern part of the chancel if the chancel is divided into two parts, one for the altar and the other for a liturgical choir. The altar section is the sanctuary. Sometimes the term sanctuary is applied to the whole church building, but this is to misuse the word. Sanctuary is to be used specifically of the altar area within a church building.

A *choir* is a room in which the choir is located. There are two kinds of choirs, liturgical choirs and congregational choirs. In cathedrals and in abbey churches where the Divine Office is sung daily, a choir of clergymen or monks is situated in a section of the chancel immediately west of the sanctuary. This is called a liturgical choir, and the section of the chancel in which it is located is called the choir. The chancel then consists of two parts, a sanctuary and a choir. In parish churches the choir, usually composed entirely of lay people, is called a congregational choir. Its assigned area in the church is also called a choir. If its place is in a loft at the west end of the nave, it is called a choir loft or gallery.

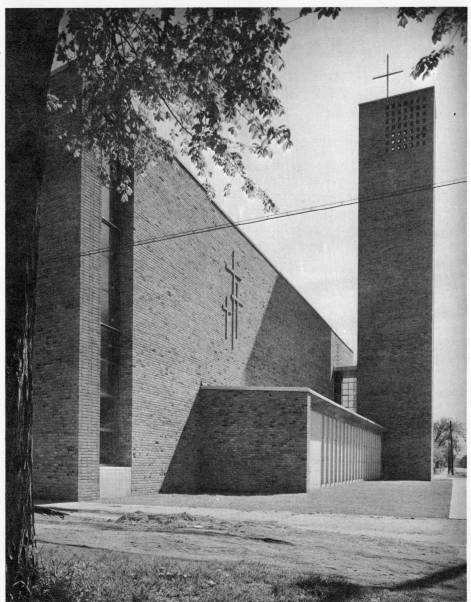

Eliel Saarinen, Architect.   Photo: George M. Ryan Studios, Minneapolis

A good example of contemporary church architecture

The baptismal font is usually located in the nave, near either the narthex or the chancel, but if the font is set in a separate room adjoining the nave, the room in which it stands is called the *baptistry*.

If a church building is cruciform, i. e., designed and built with a ground plan in the shape of a cross, the rectangular room comparable to the cross-beam of a cross is called the transept. Just as we speak of the arms of a cross, so we may also speak of the transept's projecting ends as its arms.

The *sacristy* is a special room for the clergy. In it are kept the clergy vestments and all other things necessary for service at the altar. The sacristy should have a door directly to the chancel and should be accessible from the outside without going through the church. In small churches the sacristy usually serves also as a storage room for the paraments and whatever

48

else the altar guild and acolytes need for their work. But larger churches usually have a separate room adjoining the chancel for the use of the altar guild and acolytes. Such a room is sometimes called a *working sacristy*.

A chancel which is semicircular and vaulted with a half dome is called an *apse*.

A *tower* is a structure reaching higher than the rest of the church building. It may or may not be attached to the church itself. If it has a belfry and spire, the whole is called a steeple. The simplest form of tower is a bellcote, a wall of the building carried upward with one or more arched openings for bells.

A part of a church used for minor services and devotions is sometimes called a *chapel*. The same term is applied to a small church, a college church, and a private church.

Passageways in the rooms of a church are called *aisles*. The nave usually has a center aisle from the west door to the chancel and may also have side aisles paralleling the center aisle.

Covered aisles or hallways connecting rooms of a church are called *ambulatories*. A covered passageway outside the church and open to the air is called a *cloister*.

Styles of Architecture and Ornaments

The church did not prevent the development of new styles of church architecture and ornamentation in the past; neither does it prevent or in principle discourage such developments in the present. But whatever the style, it must serve the purposes of the church's worship which we outlined briefly at the beginning of this chapter, and it must distinguish the church building from other buildings as the house of God.

For the altar guild a change of architectural style may necessitate the adaptation of traditional furnishings. For example, the paraments for an oblong or round altar will have to be cut to fit such an altar. The frontal and superfrontal may have to be made to extend all the way around the altar, especially if the chancel rail encircles the entire sanctuary, i. e., the whole area where the altar stands. The fair linen may have to be cut to fit only the top of the mensa without hanging down at the ends of the altar. The decorations on the paraments may also have to be modified or redesigned to harmonize with the new style. But as long as the basic requirements of church architecture and ornamentation are maintained, a change of style should present no serious problems for the altar guild. Major stylistic changes may require ingenuity in adapting traditional fittings for consistency in the worship setting, but such problems are by no means insurmountable and may best be accepted by designers and altar guild members as welcome challenges for the consecrated application of their special skills.

Contemporary altar crucifix

Emil Homolka, Stuttgart, Germany

CHAPTER IX

About the Altar and Its Ornaments

The Altar

The altar is the center of the church's worship. It is not a piece of church furniture like the pulpit or lectern; it is a monument. God prescribed the altar for worship in the Old Testament, and in both the Old and the New Testament era the church's worship has been at and around an altar. The altar is so central and so sacred that it has been said: "The altar is the church; the church is the altar."

The Altar's Symbolism and Significance

The altar is a symbol of God's gracious presence in His church. Its significance is that of sacrifice. It signifies primarily the sacrifice of our Lord Jesus Christ for the redemption of the world. It also signifies our sacrifice of self, prayer, praise, thanksgiving, and possessions to God through Christ, our Mediator and High Priest. The altar is also the Lord's table for the preparation, consecration, and distribution of the bread which is the holy body and the cup which is the precious blood of Christ in the Sacrament of the Altar.

Rationalists, pietists, and many Protestants deny the symbolism and significance of the altar and have either discarded it or reduced it to a mere table or only a shelf on which to put things. They have robbed the altar of its true meaning both in their theology and in their practice. Lutherans do not share their beliefs, although some churches have been influenced by their practices or by architects who prescribed for Lutheran clients buildings peculiarly appropriate for their practices. In the Lutheran Church the altar is a monument which is built from the ground up or rests on the floor. A shelf jutting from the chancel wall without legs or attachment to the floor can hardly represent a monument or suggest the symbolism and significance of the altar. The meaning and sacredness of the altar also demand reverent respect for its purpose and use. It should not be designed or used as a cupboard for tucking sacred vessels, candles, or trivia out of sight. If a choir takes its stand in the front of the church, it should not hide the altar, nor should the singers have their backs to the altar. When a projector screen is used, it should stand to the side of the altar, not in front of it. It is important that all our church practices be consistent with the meaning, dignity, and sacredness of the altar. Members of the altar guild should always remember that the altar is a monument of God's presence and that reverence and honor toward the altar are reverence and honor to God Himself and not to the wood and stone of which the altar is constructed.

The Position of the Altar

The altar occupies the most honored position in the church. It stands on the highest floor in the sanctuary or chancel. This floor is called the *footpace* or *predella*. The floor of the rest of the chancel is lower and is called the *pavement*. The altar is made to appear monumental, not only by its position and shape but also by its ornaments, linens, and paraments. If the altar is in a freestanding position so that it can be approached from all sides, its dignity will be enhanced. The altar guild must be careful that nothing is done to attract attention away from the altar. All decorations and furnishings in the chancel should be kept subordinate to it. They should help to emphasize the dignity of the altar and not detract or distract from it.

The Top of the Altar

The top of the altar is called the *mensa*. A stone altar will, of course, have a stone mensa, but traditionally even a wooden altar has a tablet of stone as its mensa. The mensa properly has five Greek crosses incised in its upper surface, one cross in the center and one near each of its four corners. The crosses represent our Lord's five crucifixion wounds in hands, feet, and side. Thus the altar's significance in commemorating the atoning sacrifice of Christ is carved on its mensa.

The Altar Crucifix

The most important ornament of the altar is the crucifix, a cross with a corpus on it. The crucifix emphasizes the incarnation of Christ and His atoning sacrifice. A plain or empty cross lacks this emphasis. Some say that the plain cross stands for the Resurrection. Be that as it may, it can also represent a devaluation of the Incarnation and a spiritualizing of Christ. The Lutheran Church, however, believes that "apart from this man there is no God."[1] Christ is incarnate and is still present with us also according to His human nature. He gives us His true body and blood in the Lord's Supper. Many Reformed and Protestant churches deny the bodily presence of Christ. According to their tradition a plain or empty cross is preferable as an expression of faith. Therefore the crucifix may become a confessional matter, although that is not always the case, and the altar guild should not make an issue of it. But the altar guild should understand why, in Lutheran tradition, an altar crucifix is preferable to a bare cross.

To be devotional, in the church any such object as a crucifix, painting, or sculpture should not be starkly realistic but rather conventional and traditional. It is not pity for Christ's suffering on Calvary that the crucifix should evoke from us, but rather mourning over our sins and gratitude for the love of God. If it does that, it has devotional character. The same thing applies to pictures, statues, and other objects in the church.

Crucifixes are of two major types. One type portrays only the sacrifice

[1] Formula of Concord, Solid Declaration VIII 81; *The Book of Concord: The Confessions of the Evangelical Lutheran Church,* trans. and ed. Theodore G. Tappert in collaboration with Jaroslav Pelikan, Robert H. Fischer, Arthur C. Piepkorn (Philadelphia: Muhlenberg Press, 1959), p. 607.

Crucifix

Crucifix

of Christ on Calvary and His priestly office. The other is more symbolic and represents our Lord in the vestments of His prophetic, priestly, and kingly offices, reigning over the cross. Both types are suitable for an altar crucifix.

The altar crucifix and candlesticks may stand on the mensa itself. Usually they are set higher on a *gradine* at the back of the mensa. The gradine may have a raised base for the crucifix so that the candlesticks stand on a lower level. The tops of the candlesticks should never be higher than the arms of the crucifix; the candles set in the candlesticks should not be higher than the crucifix. In some churches the crucifix is hung on the east wall above the center of the altar. Where the custom of celebrating toward the people from the east side of the altar is followed, the crucifix is sometimes suspended from the ceiling or placed in a high floor standard about 3 feet behind the altar.

Altar Candles

For the celebration of the Holy Communion service, at least two candles traditionally stand at the back of the altar, one on the extreme right and the other on the extreme left end. These are called *Eucharistic lights*. But if the two are the only candles ever placed on the altar, their use need not be restricted to the chief service. They may be lighted at every service.

Lighted candles are a symbol of Christ as the Light of the world. They also express the glory and joy of our holy religion. In the chief service Christ the Light comes to us in both Word and sacrament. This may be the reason for the traditional minimum of two lights for the celebration of Holy Communion. Since light also expresses glory, joy, and festivity, it is customary to increase and decrease the number of candles according to the joyfulness and solemnity of the feasts and seasons of the church year. This principle is sometimes expressed even in the kind of candlesticks set on the altar. For example, for festive Easter and Eastertide candlesticks of brass may be used, but during Lent, at least during Passiontide and Holy Week, wood candlesticks may replace the brass.

Other candles may be placed on the altar in addition to the minimum pair of Eucharistic lights. The additional candles are called *office lights*. They may be either candlesticks or candelabra. If candelabra are used, they properly have three, five, or seven branches.

All altar candles may be lighted for the Holy Communion service, but for minor services the Eucharistic lights are not used. Placing a total of six candles on the altar is hardly the best Lutheran practice, though this number is occasionally found on Lutheran altars. When the custom of using six candlesticks on the altar is followed, a problem arises at minor services. If the end candles are regarded as Eucharistic lights, only four are left for lighting at minor services. But it does not look good to have four candles burning on the altar. Perhaps the best solution is to designate all six candles office lights and to use all of them at minor services. For the Holy Communion service, two candlesticks of a different height may be set at the sides of the crucifix temporarily as Eucharistic lights.

Traditionally the altar lights are at least 51 percent beeswax. It is preferable not to use candle burners on the altar, especially not the brass type. The altar guild will replace the candles when they are burned down to 1″ or 2″ of the candlestick and wipe off the new candles to remove all finger marks. The wicks should be trimmed before every service and made to stand up so that they can be lighted easily.

All lights that stand on or near the altar should be real candles. Candles give off a vibrant, living light like wood burning in a fireplace. One never tires of looking at it. When people place lights on their dinner table, they would hardly think of using electric lights.

A burning candle also has symbolical value. Because it consumes itself in burning, it is a symbol of how our Lord spent Himself to redeem us and how we are to spend ourselves in loving service to God and man. People will probably have to be told of this significance before they become aware of it. But even without such information, candles will leave a salutary impression on them almost unconsciously. Nothing like that can ever be said of an electric bulb.

The use of other candles and lights in church will be discussed in Chapter xv, pp. 95—101.[2]

Missal Stand

The altar service book is usually placed on a missal stand. The name of the stand is derived from the book called the missal. During the Middle Ages this book contained everything necessary for the rite of the Mass. Today we call it the altar service book, but the expression missal stand has been retained.

The missal stand is a cushion or a low bookstand. A wooden stand may be used for the penitential season of Lent and a metal stand for the rest of the year. It is wise to cover a metal stand with a cloth as protection against undue wear on the cover of the altar book.

In its proper position on the altar, the front edge of the missal stand is parallel to the front edge of the mensa. It stands at an angle toward the celebrant only when it is placed on the Gospel side next to the corporal during the celebration of Holy Communion.

The Reredos

The reredos (rer' dos), dorsal, riddels, and baldachin or canopy (also called ciborium or tester) are used to give the altar a proper setting. When a diamond or other precious stone is set in a ring, it is mounted on a beautiful setting. Why? Certainly not to detract from the diamond or stone but to make it stand out, to place it in a fitting surrounding, and to enhance its beauty. Likewise the altar is given a proper setting to emphasize all the more its central and monumental place in the church.

When such a setting is a screen or ornamental work of carved stone

---

[2] A discussion of altar linens and paraments, which might logically follow here, has been reserved for a separate chapter, pp. 80—84.

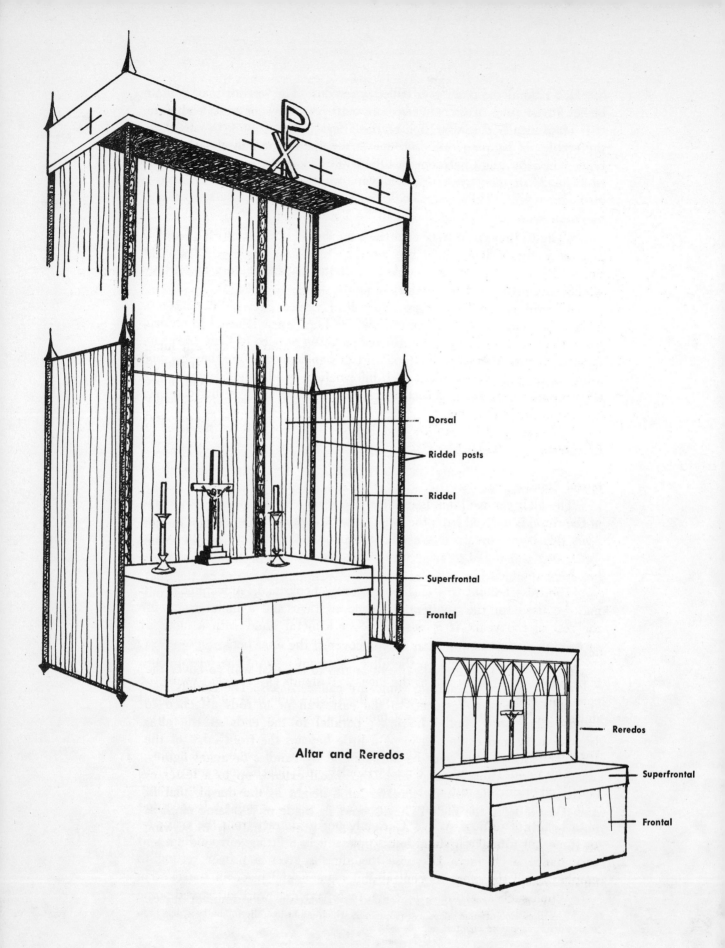

Dorsal

Riddel posts

Riddel

Superfrontal

Frontal

Altar and Reredos

Reredos

Superfrontal

Frontal

or wood behind the altar, it is called a reredos. The reredos may contain niches for statuary and paintings. It may be simple or very elaborate. It is often attached to the back of the altar. If the altar is freestanding, the reredos is built up three or four feet behind it. Some churches also have a clear passage between the back of the reredos or dorsal and the east wall of the church.

The Triptych

Another type of reredos is a triptych or even a polytych. Such a reredos is made of panels decorated with paintings and/or carvings. The side panels are hinged to fold shut over the center panel and so hide the bright colors during Holy Week, when they might be inappropriate.

The Dorsal

A simpler and less expensive setting for the altar is a curtain hung behind the altar. This curtain is called a dorsal. It is best made of a heavier-bodied fabric so that it will hang well. It need not extend more than 4' above the altar and about 1' beyond the ends of the altar. Usually it is suspended from a rod attached to the east wall of the church and may hang straight or in folds.

Care must be exercised in the choice of color and decoration. Some churches prefer to change the dorsal with the paraments of the altar. In that case the material should be the same as the paraments. If one permanent dorsal is used, the color should not clash with any of the parament colors. A deep red or gold or a tapestry in churchly design will harmonize with all the colors. A decorated dorsal is usually made with contrasting materials and colors. Three or five orphreys or panels are sewed on the basic material and edged with galloons. Before the altar guild attempts making a dorsal, it should study books on the subject and consult a good architect and decorator.

Riddels

If the dorsal is extended at right angles to the east wall to cover the ends of the altar, the resulting wings are called riddels. The riddels may be hung on brackets fastened to the east wall or to rods attached to riddel posts. They should be hung parallel to the ends of the altar about 1' away and extending to or a little beyond the front edge of the altar. The riddel posts may be surmounted by candles or angel figures. Except in large churches and when the dorsal extends up to a tester or baldachin, the riddels should be the same height as the dorsal, that is, from 6' to 8' from the floor. They should be made of the same cloth as the dorsal. A practical purpose of riddels is to prevent drafts from blowing out or guttering the candles on the altar.

The Baldachin

A canopy over the altar is called a baldachin, ciborium, or tester. It gives dignity and prominence to the altar much as does a canopy over a king's throne. The baldachin may be an architectural structure. Sometimes it is attached to the top of the dorsal. Then it is made of the same material as the dorsal or of cloth of gold. The material is stretched over a wooden frame and may be edged at the bottom with a gold silk fringe. The baldachin is properly as wide as the dorsal and as deep as the riddels. It is fastened to the east wall or to a frame from which the dorsal is suspended. The baldachin should be mounted directly above the altar.

Cleaning the Altar and Its Ornaments

Traditionally the altar is stripped and washed after the Maundy Thursday Holy Communion service. The work is done at this time not only for the practical reason that the altar needs a thorough cleansing at least once a year but also for a symbolical reason. After Maundy Thursday and before His crucifixion, our Lord was stripped of His clothes. This act was part of His deep humiliation for us and should incite us to humility, as it is written: "Let this mind be in you which was also in Christ Jesus, who, being in the form of God, thought it not robbery to be equal with God but made Himself of no reputation and took upon Him the form of a servant and was made in the likeness of men, and being found in fashion as a man, He humbled Himself and became obedient unto death, even the death of the cross. Wherefore God also hath highly exalted Him and given Him a name which is above every name, that at the name of Jesus every knee should bow of things in heaven and things in earth and things under the earth and that every tongue should confess that Jesus Christ is Lord, to the glory of God the Father" (Phil. 2:5-11). The altar may then be left bare till Easter Eve. But if it is an altar decorated with carvings and color, it should be vested with black paraments.

Keeping the altar and the entire chancel clean at all times is, of course, part of the regular work of an altar guild. It should not be necessary for the sexton to enter this part of the church. The floor of the chancel must be swept and sometimes scrubbed. The reredos of the altar and all the furniture must be dusted. The dorsal, riddels, and baldachin should be brushed lightly. The woodwork, carvings, and furniture should be closely inspected for dust and spider webs to be removed.

The altar crucifix, candlesticks, and all brasses should be cleaned with care. They should be handled with a clean cloth and not with bare hands. If the brasses are lacquered, they will not need polishing. But if they are bare metal, they should be cleaned and polished often with a good grade of metal polish and a soft cloth. This work should be done not in the chancel but in the work room. Wax drippings may be removed with hot water or by rubbing with a cloth. They should not be scratched off with the fingernails or any sharp instrument which will mark the brass. The use of hot water may also be harmful when cleaning lacquered brass. After the brasses have been cleaned and polished, they should be returned to their places in the chancel. It is well to look at the altar and its ornaments carefully before leaving, to make sure that everything is arranged correctly and that the candles are standing straight.

CHAPTER X

About the Chancel, Baptistry, and Sacristies

The Chancel

Because the altar is located in the chancel, it is the most important room in the church. It is also the room of primary concern to the altar guild. Almost all the guild's work is related to things used in the chancel.

The Pulpit

Generally the pulpit stands on or just beyond the line of demarcation between chancel and nave. In large churches it is sometimes well within the nave. The pulpit is more than just a practical piece of furniture. It symbolizes the authority of the church to preach the Word of God. Sometimes a crucifix is hung near the pulpit to emphasize that the central truth of all preaching is Christ crucified. The pulpit may stand on either the Epistle or the Gospel side of the church.

The Lectern

In most churches a lectern stands on a line with the pulpit on the opposite side of the church. Since the lectern is not needed for all church services, it may be made portable. The lectern is not needed in the Holy Communion service, when the Epistle and Gospel are read from the horns of the altar. As you face the altar, the Epistle horn is the end of the altar to your right and the Gospel horn is the end to your left. The lectern desk is sometimes in the shape of an eagle to symbolize the flight of the Gospel throughout the world.

The Chancel Rail

If the chancel is not divided into sanctuary and choir, the chancel rail is properly located on the line which divides the chancel from the nave; otherwise it is on the line of demarcation between choir and sanctuary. At the rail the communicants stand or kneel to receive the Sacrament of the Altar. There worshipers come also for other purposes, such as bringing the offerings, being confirmed, and entering holy matrimony. Going to the rail means going to the altar. In Lutheran churches the rail has an opening in front of the altar which may be closed at times with a gate or bar. In some large churches the rail surrounds three or all four sides of the sanctuary and has openings on all sides. It is nearly always provided with cushions for comfort in kneeling. The altar guild is to dust the rail, especially its carving or grillwork, and keep the cushions clean.

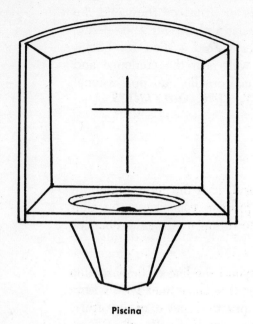

Piscina

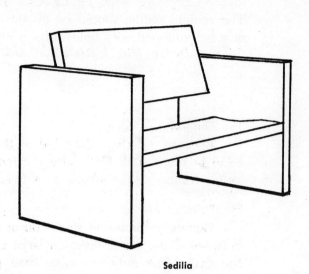

Sedilia

Credence table

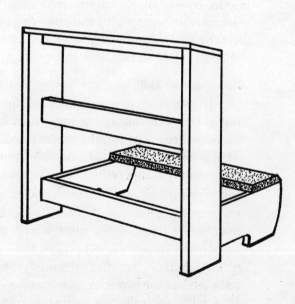

Prie-dieu

Clergy and Acolyte Seats

Chancel seats for the clergy, acolytes, or other assistants are called *sedilia*. They stand against the north and south walls. They are usually simple benches or chairs without high backs or arms, or they may be low-back pews. In front of the seats, especially those for the clergy, may be kneeling desks equipped with a kneeler and a shelf for books. The acolyte sedilia should be on the south wall near the credence and may be equipped with holders for a processional crucifix and processional candles. It is important not only that the altar guild keep the sedilia clean and dusted but also that all books, papers, and other articles be kept in order and in their proper places.

The Credence

A table or shelf against the south wall of the chancel, near the altar and for the purpose of serving the altar, is called a credence. On it the sacred vessels containing the bread, wine, and water for the Holy Communion service are placed before they are moved to the altar during the Offertory. If a lavabo basin or bowl is used, it also rests on the credence. The credence should not be used before the General Prayer as a resting place for the receptacles in which the people's offerings are collected. Once gathered, the offerings of the people belong on the altar, for they are tokens of the people's offering of themselves on the altar in thanksgiving to God. The credence should be covered at all times with a clean linen cloth similar to the fair linen on the altar. In some churches two small candlesticks stand on the credence for use during the Holy Communion service. Outside this service nothing should be on the credence except the linen cloth.

Individual Cups

In parishes in which individual Communion cups are used, the altar guild should take care of them with the same reverence as in the care of the chalice and flagon. If the cups are made of silver, they should be cleansed like the chalice. Glass cups, however, should be boiled for at least 20 minutes. The cups should be wiped dry individually with a clean linen towel and returned to the cup tray or container.*

Cleaning and Polishing the Sacred Vessels

All the sacred vessels need frequent cleaning and polishing. They should be washed in warm water and dried with a soft linen towel. If they are tarnished, they should be polished with a good grade of silver polish. Care must be taken not to scratch the surface. Wax can be removed with hot water. Flannel treated to protect against tarnishing is available. Bags should be made of such material for the sacred vessels and each vessel kept in a protective bag when not in use. When the bags become soiled, they should be washed by hand with warm water and soap.

The altar guild should not place the sacred vessels on the altar or

* The Lutheran liturgy does not envision the use of individual Communion cups, but if they are used, see Paul H. D. Lang, *Ceremony and Celebration* (St. Louis: Concordia Publishing House, 1965), p. 46.

remove them before or after church while members of the congregation are in the nave.

Floor Candlesticks and Candelabra

Floor candelabra with three, five, or seven lights, one standing at each end of the altar, are quite common in Lutheran churches. But floor candlesticks are also used in the chancel to add to the expression of joy on Sundays and feast days. Two of these may stand on the pavement on either side before the altar. Floor candlesticks may also be employed in funeral and wedding services. We shall discuss sconces and sanctuary lamps in the chapter on the use of lights in the church.

The Prie-Dieu

A prie-dieu is a litany or prayer desk. In some churches it is placed in the center of the nave in front of the chancel just for the praying of the Litany. Since the Litany is a penitential office, the minister descends into the nave of the church to read it, in allusion to Joel 2:17: "Let the priests, the ministers of the Lord, weep between the porch and the altar, and let them say: Spare Thy people, O Lord." The prie-dieu, however, is also used in the chancel and in the sacristy. It is very desirable and convenient for the saying of confessions, prayers, and devotions.

The Piscina

The piscina is a basin built into the south wall of the chancel near the credence or somewhere in the sacristy and equipped with a drain running directly to the soil. It is used for the reverent disposal of the consecrated wine left over from the Holy Communion service and of the water with which the chalice, flagon, and cruets are cleansed, as well as of the water used in Holy Baptism. It would not be proper to pour these elements into a common drain. If the church is not equipped with a piscina, the vessels may be carried outside and their contents poured on the ground.

The Baptismal Font

Next to the altar, the baptismal font, also called simply the font, is the most important object in the church's worship. It really does not belong to the chancel and its furnishings, for it stands either in a separate room called a baptistry or in the nave. Holy Baptism is the sacrament of incorporation or entrance into the body of Christ, the church. To symbolize this entrance and incorporation, the font is often placed near the main entrance to the church. But in Lutheran churches it stands more often near the entrance to the chancel. This position brings Holy Baptism into close relation with the Sacrament of the Altar. But wherever the font is placed, it should not detract from the centrality and prominence of the altar.

The font is usually octagonal in shape; it may stand on a low octagonal platform. Since Christ rose from the dead on the first day of the week, also designated the eighth day, the number eight is considered a symbol of regeneration, the new birth from spiritual death to spiritual life.

Holy Baptism is a sacrament which Christ gave to His church, and it is desirable that whenever possible, the congregation participate in its administration. The concern of the altar guild will be the preparation of the font and the things needed for the sacrament before the church service in which it is to be administered. After the service the guild will dispose of the baptismal water, wash the linen towels that were used, and set the font and its surroundings in order.

THE SACRISTIES

The Clergy Sacristy

A church office for the pastor and a secretary, equipped with a typewriter and filing cabinets, is not a proper clergy sacristy and has no place next to the chancel. A clergy sacristy is a sacred room adjoining the chancel, in which the clergymen put on their vestments and devoutly prepare themselves for doing their parts in the divine services of the church. Therefore it should be equipped with suitable cabinets for clerical vestments, a table, chairs, a prie-dieu, a crucifix, and a pair of candlesticks. In small churches a clergy sacristy and a working sacristy for the altar guild are often combined. When such is the case, the altar guild members and the acolytes must do their work at such time and in such manner that they do not disturb the pastor in his devotions immediately before the service.

The Working Sacristy

The working sacristy is a separate room especially for the altar guild and acolytes. It may adjoin the clergy sacristy or be on the opposite side of the chancel. If it is on the opposite side, an ambulatory should be provided behind the chancel so that it will not be necessary to cross the chancel to get from one sacristy to the other.

The working sacristy should have more than ample room for work and storage. It should have a cabinet where all paraments may be hung without folding. It should have cupboards for fair linens, corporals, burses, purificators, palls, baptismal and lavabo towels, and many other linens; and storage places for candles, candlesticks, torches, candlelighters, crucifixes, a supply of wine and wafers, and the sacred vessels. The working sacristy should have a fairly large table, a sink with hot and cold running water, and all things necessary for laundering, drying, and ironing the linens and vestments. Suitable facilities must be provided for cleaning the brasses, for polishing the sacred vessels, and for arranging flowers. A piscina is needed, even if the chancel has one, for cleaning and washing the sacred vessels and linens which come in contact with the elements used in the sacraments. A good calendar which provides all necessary information about the days and seasons of the church year should hang on the wall along with framed illustrations, instructions, and prayers. On one wall should be a crucifix, in front of it a prie-dieu and beside it a wall bracket with candlesticks. A closet for clothes and vestments is also necessary, as well as storage space for such seasonal objects as the Christmas crèche, Advent wreath frame and standard, paschal candlestick and candle, pew-end candleholders and flower containers, and window candleholders.

By its appearance and atmosphere the working sacristy should reflect reverence and devotion. It should not be made to look feminine by hanging domestic drapes on the windows or by putting up decorations which cause it to look like a room in a home.

One member of the altar guild should be appointed to be responsible for keeping the working sacristy clean and in order. She need not do the work herself, but she should see to it that the work is done. It would be her duty to initiate a proper storage system if this has not been done. This system would provide a numbered list of items stored and their locations. The numbering could start at a given point and then circle the room. The complete list should be typed and posted in the room for ready reference. Everyone could then find where each item is stored and where it should be replaced. The system should furnish a continual inventory so that all supplies may conveniently be replenished as needed. It is also very important that the working sacristy be kept in such order that when a visitor is shown around the church, no apology need ever be made for its untidy appearance.

The Choir Sacristy

Somewhere near the choir's place in the church a room should be provided in which the choir can gather before the services. This room is called the choir sacristy. It should have cloak and vestment closets and dressing rooms for men and women. The room should be reverent and devotional in appearance. A crucifix should hang on a wall in a prominent place, perhaps over a piano where a short rehearsal may be held before the church service. Shelves should be provided for the orderly storage of choir music, and there should be a table and an ample number of chairs.

Keeping the choir sacristy in proper condition should not be the duty of the altar guild, but the choir vestments may be placed in the guild's care. It may be possible for the altar guild to tailor the choir vestments and keep them clean and in good repair.

CHAPTER XI

About the Sacred Vessels

For the Holy Eucharist

The sacred vessels used in the celebration of the Holy Communion service are the chalice, the paten, the ciborium or pyx, the flagon, the spoon, the water and wine cruets, and the lavabo bowl. The last three vessels are not used everywhere. If possible, all the vessels, with the exception of the glass cruets and the lavabo bowl, should be sterling silver lined with gold. They may also be solid gold and richly ornamented. Some contemporary ornamentation in enamel is very good.

The *chalice* is the single cup which our Lord blessed and from which all drank when He instituted the Sacrament of the Altar. It is also called the cup of blessing, the cup of the Lord, the common cup, and the Communion cup.

The *paten* is the plate for the bread. It is made to fit into the mouth or rim of the chalice and large enough so that it can be used for the distribution. It is the symbol of the "one bread" broken in pieces. These pieces are called *wafers* or *hosts*.

The *ciborium* or *pyx* is the container for additional wafers. The ciborium has the shape of a covered chalice and the pyx that of a round covered box, also called a host box. Sometimes the ciborium is used for the distribution in place of the paten, but in that case the paten is still used for the consecration.

The *flagon* is a container for additional wine. Large cruets are sometimes used in place of a flagon.

The *spoon* is only a tool which is needed very rarely. It is used for the removal of pieces of cork or other matter that may have fallen into the wine.

The *cruet* is a glass container for water or wine, with a stopper in the shape of a cross. Wine cruets used in place of a flagon are usually much larger than water cruets. A water cruet is used for pouring a little water into the chalice where the traditional mixed chalice (wine mixed with a little water) is retained and where the celebrant cleanses or purifies the chalice and paten ceremonially after the distribution. It is also used with the lavabo ceremony.

The *lavabo bowl* holds the water for the ceremonial cleansing of the celebrant's fingers after the offerings of the people (including the bread and wine) are placed on the altar. The ceremony is purely symbolical and is connected with the words of Psalm 26:6, 7: "I will wash mine hands in innocency; so will I compass Thine altar, O Lord, that I may publish with the voice of thanksgiving and tell of all Thy wondrous works."

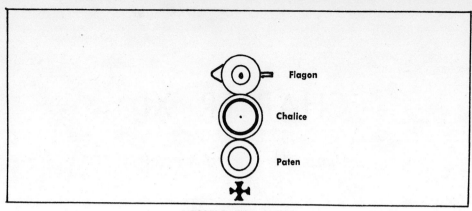

Flagon

Chalice

Paten

VESSELS ON ALTAR

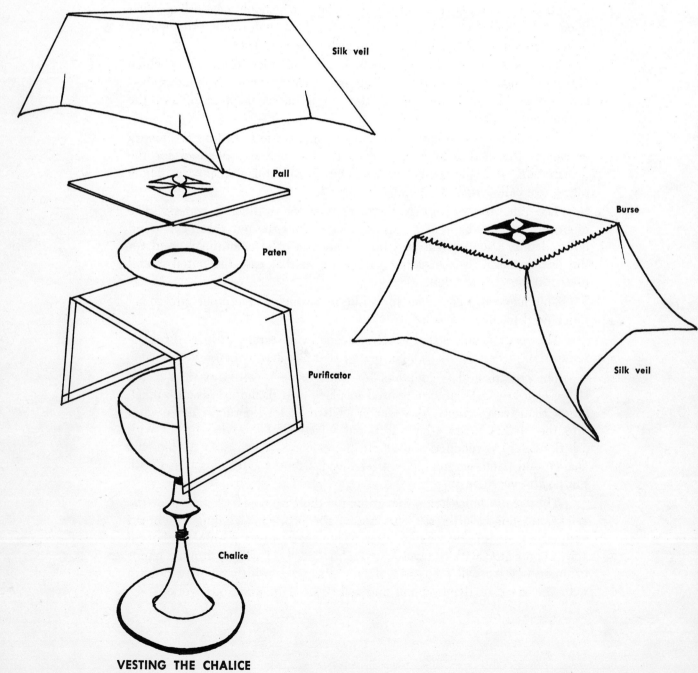

Silk veil

Pall

Paten

Purificator

Chalice

Burse

Silk veil

VESTING THE CHALICE

For Holy Baptism

In the administration of the sacrament of Holy Baptism, the sacred vessels used are the bowl of the baptismal font or the baptismal bowl and the ewer.

The *baptismal bowl* is the bowl part of the font, a removable bowl for water in the font, or simply a bowl for water in baptism without a font.

The *ewer* is a pitcher to carry water to the font. It should be of churchly design and large enough to fill the bowl of the font. If the font does not have a drain to the ground, it is proper to remove the water from it after baptism into the ewer. The water is then poured into the piscina or on mother earth outside the church.

Arrangement of the Holy Communion Vessels

Before the Holy Communion service the chalice is veiled in the sacristy as follows: Over the mouth of the chalice lay a folded purificator to hang over the edges on the right and left sides. On it lay the paten, and cover the paten with the pall. Then cover all with the chalice veil, and lay the burse, containing the corporal, a supply of purificators, and the post-Communion veil, on the chalice veil.

If the veiled chalice is placed on the altar by the pastor before the service, the corporal is taken out of the burse and placed on the fair linen in the midst of the altar. The veiled chalice is put on the corporal, and the burse is set upright against the gradine close to the left of the chalice. The other vessels usually remain on the credence until the Offertory. But when these, too, are placed on the altar before the service, the flagon stands on the corporal behind and to the right of the veiled chalice, and the ciborium stands on the corporal behind and to the left (Gospel side) of the veiled chalice.

When the chalice is unveiled during the Offertory, the position of the sacred vessels on the corporal is paten or ciborium on the center forepart of the corporal, chalice behind the paten or ciborium, and wine cruets or flagon behind the chalice. Another arrangement is to place the chalice and flagon on the Epistle side of the corporal with the chalice in front and the paten and ciborium on the Gospel side of the corporal with the paten in front.

If all the vessels except the chalice are placed on the credence, you may prepare them by filling the ciborium with wafers or hosts, the flagon with wine, and the water cruets (if used) with water. Set these on the credence, the flagon to your right and the ciborum to the left. Behind them place the water cruets and the lavabo bowl and towel, if they are used.

Arrangement of Holy Baptism Vessels

For Holy Baptism, fill the ewer with water and place it, with a separate towel for each person to be baptized, on a table or shelf near the baptismal font. After the church service, remove the water, ewer, and towels, and close the font by replacing the cover. The font and ewer should be wiped clean and the towels laundered.

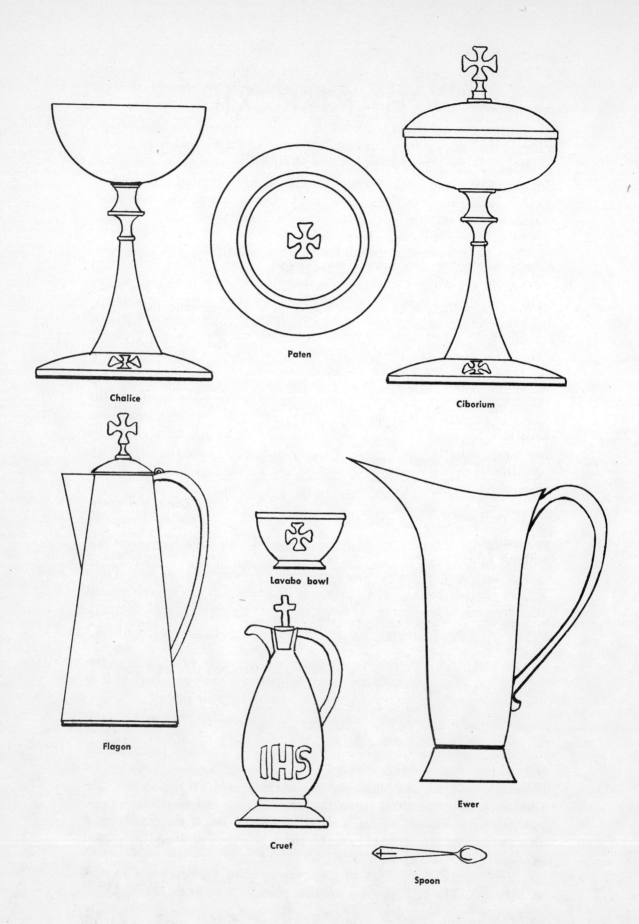

Chalice

Paten

Ciborium

Flagon

Lavabo bowl

Cruet

IHS

Ewer

Spoon

CHAPTER XII

About the Paraments

The Altar Paraments

The altar paraments include two pieces, the frontal and the superfrontal. For unconventional altars see p. 49.

The *frontal* covers the whole front of the altar from the top down to the footpace. It is the primary altar parament, the one that carries the colors of the church year, the one that is changed.

The *superfrontal* hangs down 7" to 12" from the mensa, depending on the length of the altar. Wherever the frontal is suspended from below the mensa of the altar, the purpose of the superfrontal is to cover the top of the frontal and so conceal the device which attaches the frontal to the altar. In modern design, however, this purpose of the superfrontal has been lost, for often the frontal is attached to the lowest altar cloth and the superfrontal is sewed to the top of the frontal. Like the dorsal, the superfrontal need not carry the colors of the church year and, if a neutral color, need not be changed.

Under two circumstances the superfrontal is often made the color-carrying and only altar parament. If the altar front is highly decorative or ornamental stone, wood, or metal, the facing itself serves as a frontal without fabric covering. If no fabric frontal is used, the superfrontal carries the liturgical colors. The second circumstance involves cost. Frontals are much more expensive than superfrontals, and if a church cannot afford frontals, it may make the superfrontal serve the purpose of a frontal. Nonetheless, an effort should be made to acquire a proper frontal as soon as possible.

Frontals and superfrontals should never be made to hang over the ends of the altar, only over the front, or over the front and back if it is the custom to celebrate behind the altar and facing the people.

Five sets of paraments — white, red, violet, green, and black — are sufficient for ordinary use during the church year. In general, without indicating exceptions, the white set is for high festivals and their seasons, the red for minor festivals, the violet for penitential seasons, the green for ordinary days, and the black for Good Friday only. (For details, see Chapter xvi, pp. 102–107. If the altar front is plain and the altar stripped bare for Good Friday, no black set is necessary. But if the front of the altar is ornamented, it should be covered with black paraments on Good Friday.

If it is impossible to get all the colors at once, the best color to start with is red. The red may be used in place of the white for the high

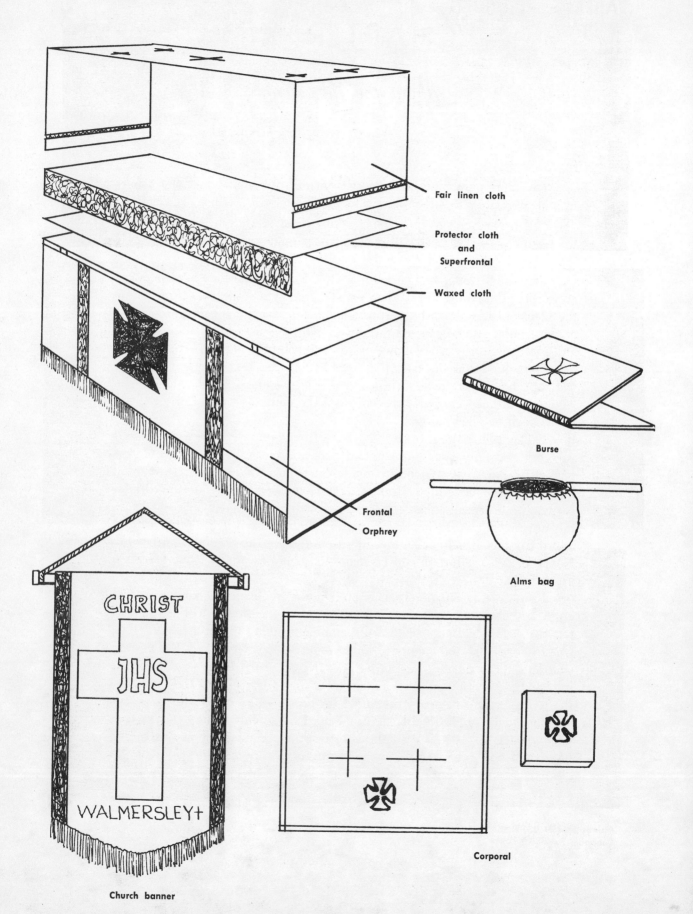

Fair linen cloth

Protector cloth
and
Superfrontal

Waxed cloth

Frontal

Orphrey

Burse

Alms bag

CHRIST
JHS
WALMERSLEY†

Church banner

Corporal

Contemporary altar paraments

festivals and the green for ordinary days, while during the penitential seasons the altar may be left bare. Later a violet set may be added. Then there will be a color suitable for all seasons. The next set might be green. This will provide red for the high and minor festivals, green for the ordinary days, and violet for the penitential seasons. Then add white and finally black sets.

The Fringe

All paraments may be edged along the bottom with a fringe, preferably a spaced silk fringe. The fringe of an altar frontal may be 2″ or 3″ deep, but that on a superfrontal only 1″ or 2″. Metallic fringe is not recommended; the fringe should be the same kind of material as the cloth of the parament. The basic idea of a fringe is that the cloth itself be fringed. If the cloth is heavy enough, a satisfactory fringe may be obtained without adding a separate band. For example, if a set of altar paraments for the penitential seasons is made of heavy unbleached linen, representing sackcloth, and is decorated with violet orphreys or symbols, the material itself may be raveled out along the bottom edge. Nothing else is needed. But ordinarily a separate band is sewn to the material. Such a fringe should be of silk and the color of the material to which it is sewn. If it is spaced fringe, it should contain the color of the material and the color or colors of the parament embroidery and orphrey decorations. The fringe's corded edge should be sewn to the back of the cloth so that only the fringe itself shows.

Pulpit and Lectern Paraments

The pulpit and lectern may also have paraments. These may be called *pulpit frontal* and *lectern frontal*, also known as falls. Their material and color may be the same as the altar frontal, or if the superfrontal does not carry the colors, they should match the superfrontal. These frontals should be wide enough to cover the pulpit and lectern desks and long enough to be in good proportion to the pulpit or lectern. Their fringes should not be more than 2″ deep.

If the pulpit or lectern desks are ornamented with carvings, no frontals are needed.

Parament Materials

If possible the paraments should be made of genuine fabrics. Synthetics and imitation materials are not desirable. The material may be plain silk, but damasks and brocades are more beautiful. The particular design woven into a damask or brocade is not too important, but it should be fitting for church use. If it embodies Christian symbols, the choice of damask will be governed by the appropriateness of the symbols for the seasons in which the damask will be used. For example, the Lily damask is suitable for the white paraments, the Ely Crown for the red, the Passion Flower for the violet, and the Tudor Rose for the green. Care should be taken in the choice of shades. The choice will depend somewhat on the amount of light in the chancel, but ordinarily true green should be chosen

Paramentenverein, St. Marienberg, Germany

Photo: Köglsperger, Helmstedt

A good example of a contemporary altar frontal

Contemporary parament design suitable for violet set

Kurt Wolff Wuppertal-Barmen, Düsseldorf, Germany

and not grass green; violet, not vivid purple; red, not American beauty; ecclesiastical white, not dead white.

The paraments may be richly embroidered, although embroidery is not necessary, except that they must have at least a cross to show their sacred use. Orphreys of cloth of gold or other contrasting materials may also be used for decorations. The materials and decorations should reflect the meaning and spirit of the days and seasons in which the paraments are used. Thus the white set should be the most ornate, the costliest, and the most beautiful, since it is used on the high feasts of the incarnation, resurrection, and ascension of our Lord. The symbols and other decorations should be in harmony with the thoughts and sentiments of these feasts. They should help teach, confess, and glorify the Christ of Christmas, Easter, and the Ascension and the great truths which these feasts and their seasons emphasize. The same applies to the other sets. The violet set, for instance, should be quite plain, and the black set should be the simplest and most solemn.

To illustrate these principles, we shall describe the five sets of paraments which one altar guild made, doing its own planning, buying, cutting, designing, sewing, and embroidering. It should be understood, of course, that these are mentioned only as examples of what can be done by a nonprofessional group of women willing to study and work at the art of making paraments. These sets represent a single choice of materials and ornamentation. For every set there is a wide choice of appropriate symbols, color combinations, and kinds of materials. Altar guilds should remember the many possibilities as they read the following descriptions.

The white set was made of pure silk damask with a fleur-de-lis design. Panels of cloth of gold, which carry a design of pomegranates and roses symbolical of Easter and Christmas, were sewed on the altar frontal. These panels are 7″ wide and edged with a white silk cord. In the center of the frontal a design consisting of the Chi-Rho and the Alpha and Omega was embroidered in light blue and edged in gold and surrounded by rays of glory in gold. The superfrontal was decorated with an embroidery of the Alleluia in gold with illuminated letters in blue. Trumpets of gold in saltire (like the letter X) were embroidered on each end. For the pulpit and lectern frontals the emblems IHC and XPC were chosen, done in gold and edged in blue. The bookmarkers were made of the same cloth of gold as the panels on the frontal. The bottom edges of all the paraments were finished with a white silk fringe, and all the frontals were lined with blue satin. This set turned out to be very rich and festive, and its symbols and ornamentations all harmonize with the high feasts and the seasons for which it is used.

The red set, used for Pentecost and many minor festivals, was made of silk velvet. Some authorities do not recommend velvet as a background material for paraments. They claim that it fades easily and soon looks shabby. While these claims are true of cheap velvet, the same can be said of other cheap materials. Therefore the use of velvet cannot be condemned on that score alone. A good silk velvet will not fade, and it certainly looks soft and rich. It must be admitted, however, that it is hard to find good

74

velvet and that it is ordinarily better to buy damask. Plush is not suitable; its nap is so deep that it cannot be decorated very well and looks coarse. Brocades and tapestries, too, are not always suitable; they are often too assertive. Brocades and tapestries may be used if they are not decorated or if only parts of the woven design are outlined with gold embroidery or cord.

However, this set was made of red silk velvet — a true red, not an off-color. A running design featuring the quatrefoil, fleur-de-lis, and trefoil was embroidered in gold outline stitch from end to end of the superfrontal. On the center of the frontal a piece of blue silk cut in the shape of a quatrefoil was appliqued after it had been embroidered with a figure of the Agnus Dei carrying a banner of victory. The Agnus Dei stands on grass and flowers against a blue background representing the sky. It was embroidered in white, the nimbus in gold with the rays in red, and the banner in white with a red cross on it. Surrounding this central figure, the frontal has embroidered symbols of the four evangelists: St. Matthew, the winged man; St. Mark, the winged lion; St. Luke, the winged ox; and St. John, the winged eagle. These were embroidered on red silk and appliqued on the velvet with a circular gold border. The ends of the frontal were finished with narrow orphreys bearing a vine-and-rose design.

The pulpit frontal was embroidered with the words "Abide in Me," a cross patée at the beginning of the sentence and a cross frette at the end. The letters were done in gold outline with heavy gold floss and the crosses in solid gold. The lectern frontal was decorated with an embroidered design, the sword and keys, symbol of St. Peter and St. Paul, surrounded by oak leaves and enclosed in a quatrefoil with points.

Silk damask was used for the green set. On the superfrontal the words "Holy, Holy, Holy" were embroidered in gold and edged in red, with the letters illuminated in red. The words were separated by crosses alisée patée enclosed in a circle. They were done in gold, edged in red, with the circles in red.

The green frontal contains three panels with three encircled symbols in each panel. The upper symbol in each panel is the triangle with inter-woven triquetras. The triquetra was embroidered in gold, the triangle in white, and the circles surrounding it in gold edged in red. Below this symbol in the first panel is the Manus Dei ("Hand of God") in white with a nimbus of gold and red rays. The gold circle around it is edged in red. Under this symbol is a six-pointed star, the symbol of creation. This was done in white with the circle around it in gold. The second panel contains the Agnus Dei as the second symbol. The Agnus is reclining on a book with seven seals. It was embroidered in white with the nimbus gold and rays red. The book was done in gold outline and the seven seals in red on cords of gold. The third figure is the redemption symbol, the anchor with a cross in saltire. The anchor was embroidered in gold and the cross in white. Under the first symbol in the third panel is the Spiritus Sanctus (the dove) embroidered in white with a gold nimbus and red rays. The third symbol shows the sevenfold gifts of the Holy Spirit falling in the form of seven flames on a globe, an emblem of the earth. The flames were embroidered in red and gold and the globe in white. All these symbols are surrounded with a gold circle edged in red. Thus the truths stated in the three articles of the Apostles' Creed are portrayed in the three panels of this frontal.

The pulpit frontal was decorated with a circle and triquetra design. The lectern frontal was ornamented with a triangle and interwoven circle. Both were embroidered in gold and edged in red. All the frontals of the green set were finished with a spaced fringe in green and gold.

The violet set was made of heavy natural (unbleached) linen, which represents sackcloth. The words "Behold the Lamb of God" were embroidered in violet on the superfrontal, with pointed Greek crosses in violet on each end. The frontal was ornamented with alternating rows of passion crosses and roses of Sharon (Advent and Messianic rose). The crosses are violet and the roses red. Both the frontal and superfrontal were finished on the bottom with a fringe of the material itself. The pulpit and lectern are left bare during Advent and Lent, and therefore these frontals were omitted.

The black set was made very plain. The superfrontal was not ornamented at all. The frontal was decorated with only a crown of thorns and three nails done in silver outline stitch. The material itself was fringed on the lower edge. The set has no pulpit and lectern frontals.

These descriptions illustrate the principles which underlie the choice of materials and ornamentation for the paraments. Under ordinary circumstances it is not advisable for the altar guild to make such elaborate paraments. If the members are not very skilled in needlework, properly equipped to do the work, and somewhat experienced, the results will not be satisfactory. Amateurs will find that it is cheaper and more gratifying to have the paraments made than to attempt the work themselves. They may waste much costly material by mistakes, both in cutting and in embroidery, and in the end the result will be faulty and disappointing.

In buying paraments it will be necessary to exercise great care. Many commercial firms do not produce pieces that are liturgically correct in design, materials, and workmanship. Many of the commercial houses are more interested in sales than in church art. Consequently it is important to deal with firms and guilds which have knowledgeable and skilled workers.

The first requirement for paraments is good design. Therefore it is well to have them designed by an artist. Even fine needlework cannot compensate for poor composition of line and color. Paraments should be artistic, and all the symbols and decorations ought to be in harmony with the purpose for which each parament is to be used. A second requirement is that the paraments be made of genuine, not imitation, materials. Third, all needlework should be handwork. Machine sewing and embroidery lack the quality of devotion and beauty expressed in handwork.

The fact that paraments should generally be purchased and made to order by competent workers does not mean that an altar guild cannot, in time, learn the art of making them. It will take much study, time, and practice, but it can be done. Good books are available which give detailed instructions on design, materials and tools, mounting frames, tracing patterns, the various kinds of embroidery stitches, and how to do them. Such books are a "must" for altar guilds which want to undertake the work of making their own paraments. They contain the information needed and give illustrations with scale drawings for cutting, mounting, and embroidering. The altar guild should also seek the advice and help of people who are thoroughly familiar with church needlework. Church needlewomen can be found in metropolitan areas who will give instructions to altar guilds and from whom individuals can take lessons.

We would like to encourage all altar guilds to learn how to make their own paraments and vestments. However, they must be content at first to devote themselves to study and practice. After they have acquired sufficient skill, they should start with something simple, like a stole, a chalice veil, or an acolyte cotta. It is not wise to undertake anything very difficult at the beginning, especially very much embroidery. Most beginners attempt making paraments which are too decorative and have too many symbols. It is more satisfactory to begin with paraments made of inexpensive materials and with a few simple decorations. These can be replaced later with paraments and vestments made of more costly materials and ornamented with more embroidery.

Fastening the Paraments

The altar, pulpit, and lectern frontals are attached to lining material or heavy linen which extends over the mensa of the altar and the desks of the pulpit and lectern. A wide hem may be sewed at the end of this material through which heavy flat rods are inserted to hold the frontals in place. If the mensa extends an inch or two over the front edge of the altar, the altar frontal can be hung from it with a rod. Only the superfrontal need then be attached to a piece of material that extends over the mensa.

Bookmarkers

Decorative *bookmarkers* which hang down over the pulpit and lectern desks are often made to match the material and color of the frontal. They should not be more than 3″ or 4″ wide. The ends may have a fringe and the markers may be decorated with embroidery. Bookmarkers that are actually used in the altar, pulpit, and lectern books should only be ½″ wide and be made of grosgrain ribbon. They are not decorated or fringed. Often five ribbons, one each of the five colors of the church year, are attached to a ring and inserted in the pages of the book.

Chalice Veils

Chalice veils are made of the same materials and colors as the altar frontals. These cover the chalice before the Offertory. The size is 18″ to 24″ square, depending on the height of the chalice. The veils are lined with silk of a contrasting color and have a cross or symbol embroidered on the center of the front part, which is exposed to the people. All four sides may have a narrow silk fringe.

Burse

Together with the chalice veil a matching silk burse is generally provided. The burse is an envelope-like case in which the corporal, purificators, and post-Communion veil are carried to the altar. The burse is about 9″ square and embroidered on one side.

An easy way to make a burse is to prepare two pieces of strong cardboard 9″ square, cut two pieces of silk 12″ square, and embroider the center of one of the pieces of silk. Then stretch each piece of silk over a piece of cardboard, fold the edges over, and lace the silk securely to the cardboard on the backside. Cover the lacing with white linen, stitching it onto the silk. Place the linen sides together and join the bottom edge with cloth hinges. They may be joined instead by sewing gussets on three sides, like a purse with the top edge open. The edges may be finished with a silk cord.

Instead of cloth hinges, 1″ hinges of the same silk cord used to finish the edges of the burse may be used. The hinges may also be attached along the bottom edge even before the linen is stitched on. Then the linen may hide both the lacing and the hinging stitches. Another way of making the hinge is to lace the two pieces of cardboard into a single piece of silk 11″ by 21″. This allows a 1″ hinge along the bottom edge and eliminates the need for separate hinging.

Altar Crucifix Veils

In some churches the altar crucifix is veiled during all of Lent or from Passion Sunday to the eve of Easter. Two veils are usually provided, violet for Lent and white for Maundy Thursday. They may be made of chiffon large enough to fall to the bottom of the crucifix and gathered about the stem near the base with a silk thread.

Lenten Veils

All pictures and ornate objects are covered in some churches during Lent or Passiontide with Lenten veils of unbleached or blue-dyed linen. This custom adds to the solemnity of the Lenten season by hiding the colorful and festive things that seem inappropriate during this time.

Banners

In the Lutheran churches of Europe, Sunday schools, societies, guilds, and brotherhoods have banners bearing symbols of our Christian faith. In American Lutheran churches, one does not see them very often. The banners are carried in processions; when not in use, they are kept in the chancel suspended from rods attached to the walls or to floor standards. For illustrations and instructions on how they are made, we suggest consulting such books as Beryl Dean's *Ecclesiastical Embroidery* or *Banners, Banners* by Anderson and Caemmerer.

Alms Bags

Alms bags for gathering the offerings may be made of silk or velvet in the colors of the church year. The size should be about 9″ by 12″. The bottom of the bag may be either rounded or pointed. The top is mounted on an oblong metal ring to which wooden handles are attached at both ends. The inside of the bags should be lined with buckram and sateen; the outside may be decorated with an embroidered cross or other suitable design. A silk cord all around will make a neat edging. Alms bags are very churchly in appearance and have many advantages over other containers for gathering the money offerings of the people. When the offerings have been gathered, the alms bags are placed on the altar on top of one another in such a way that the handles form a cross.

The Funeral Pall

The funeral pall is used to cover the casket during the service in church. It is about 8' by 12', made of black, violet, red, or white silk damask or velvet and lined with satin or silk. Appliqued on the pall may be a cross of cloth from edge to edge the length and width of the pall; if desired, the center of the cross may be embroidered with the monogram of the sacred name of Jesus, the IHC. Before the funeral service the altar guild places the pall on a table in the narthex. The pall is thrown over the coffin in the narthex before it enters the nave and is again removed in the narthex after the service. With the pall the church covers all her children alike and, by keeping the casket closed during the service, directs her worship to the altar. The coffin is properly placed in the center aisle, parallel with the aisle and feet to the altar, unless the corpse is that of a pastor. A pastor's head is placed toward the altar. The pall may be kept on a roll its full length and stored in a box for the purpose.

All other large paraments should be hung in vestment cases or laid flat in drawers when not in use. They should not be folded, for folding breaks silk fibers in time. When they become soiled, they should be dry-cleaned.

Ecclesiastical Arts Catalog
Concordia Publishing House

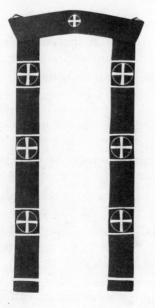

Contemporary stole

Contemporary pulpit and lectern frontal

79

CHAPTER XIII

About the Sacred Linens

Three linens cover the mensa of the altar at all times: the cere linen, the protector linen, and the fair linen.

The Cere Linen

The *cere linen* is a waxed linen the exact size of the mensa. Its purpose is to protect the upper linens from dampness which may arise from a stone mensa under certain climatic conditions. It is made of heavy linen. Melted paraffin is slowly painted over the whole linen as evenly as possible. Then the linen is ironed to spread the paraffin more evenly. If it is not placed on the altar at once, the cere linen is rolled on a cardboard roll with care to avoid wrinkles.

The Protector Linen

Over the cere linen is laid a *protector linen*. This may be the piece of heavy linen to which the superfrontal is sewn to hold it in place, or it may be a separate linen. If separate, it is exactly like the cere linen but not treated with paraffin.

The Fair Linen

The *fair linen* is placed on the protector linen. It is as wide as the mensa and extends one third or all the way to the floor at the ends. (cf. p. 49). It should be the finest linen and handled reverently, because it is symbolic of the linen which the women used to wrap the body of our Lord when He was laid in the tomb. The linen should be hemmed by hand, twenty stitches or more to the inch, not merely hemstitched; the hem should be 1″ to 2″ along the sides, 3″ to 4″ at the ends. Five flat Greek crosses should be embroidered on it with white cotton thread, four of the crosses near the corners of the mensa and the fifth in the center.

Folding the Linens

The fair linen, the protector linen, and the cere linen are removed from the altar one by one by bringing the ends together in the center, the end on the Epistle side first. Then they are folded twice again the same way, bringing the ends into the middle of the altar. This makes six foldings. Finally the two ends are brought together, making seven foldings in all. When the linens are placed on the altar, the procedure is reversed. Each linen is laid in the middle of the altar and then unfolded. If desired, these linens may be rolled instead of folded.

The Credence Linen

The credence shelf or table is covered with a *credence linen,* similar in shape to the fair linen on the altar. The linen's size depends on the size of the credence. The hems should be smaller than those of the fair linen. It should have only one cross — in the center.

Sacramental Linens

The sacred linens used for the Sacrament of the Altar are the corporal, the pall, the purificators, the white, or post-Communion, veil, and whenever used, the lavabo towel.

The Corporal

The *corporal* is the linen which is placed over the fair linen in the midst of the altar and on which the sacred Communion vessels stand. Like the fair linen, it should be handled with special reverence, because it is symbolic of the linen wrapped about the face of Christ when He was laid in the tomb. It is fair linen 20″ to 21″ square, with a small Greek cross outlined in the center about 3″ from the front edge and a ½″ hem all around. It is folded right side up in nine squares, three folds lengthwise and three crosswise. When it is not on the altar, it is kept in the burse. It should not hang over the edge of the altar when it is put in place.

The Pall

The *pall* is used to cover the top of the chalice or paten. It is made of two squares of some stiff material which will not be damaged by laundering, e. g., thin aluminum, each piece covered on one side with linen. One piece of linen is embroidered with a cross or IHC surrounded by a crown of thorns. The linen is cut 2″ larger than the plate, turned over the edges of the plate, and drawn together with long stitches from side to side both ways. Then the two covered plates are securely sewn together along the edges. The pall is usually 7″ square.

The Purificator

The *purificator* is a small napkin used to cleanse the rim of the chalice during the distribution of Holy Communion. It is an 11″ to 13″ square of medium-weight linen. A simple cross is embroidered in the center or on one end, and it is finished by hand with a ⅛″ hem all around. It is folded like the corporal, only right side out. Two or three are placed in the burse for each celebration.

The White, or Post-Communion, Veil

The *white veil,* or post-Communion veil, is used instead of the silk chalice veil to cover all the sacred vessels after the distribution. It is a 30″ to 36″ square of very fine linen veiling with a ½″ handmade hem. The center front may be decorated with embroidery, but it must be done in white and should be kept light.

The Lavabo Towel

In churches in which the lavabo ceremony is used, a *lavabo towel* is needed for each celebration of the Sacrament of the Altar. The size is

12″ by 18″. It is made of the same kind of linen as the purificator and is hemmed in the same way. A cross is embroidered at the center of one end about 3″ above the hem. The towel is folded lengthwise, right side out, in three lengths, so that it will hang evenly over the arm. When it is placed on the credence, each end is folded to the center.

For Private Communion

The sacred linens used for communicating the sick are smaller than those used in the church. The corporal is not more than 15″ square, the pall 3″, the purificator 6″, and the veil 9″. All are made of fine linen and should have a small cross.

For Holy Baptism

The traditional baptismal towel is made of medium-weight linen 18″ to 24″ square or 12″ wide and 25″ long. A cross is embroidered in the center or near one end; the hem should not be more than ½″ wide. It is folded the same way as the lavabo towel.

Some altar guilds make a small baptismal towel for presentation to each child after its baptism. The towel is made of fine linen 7″ by 13″. The lengthwise hems are made as narrow as possible and the end hems about ½″. The cross patée fitchée, symbolizing the Holy Trinity in whose name the child is baptized, or an eight-pointed star, symbolizing regeneration, may be embroidered in the center or on one end of the towel.

The Chrisom

The *chrisom*, or baptismal robe, was retained by Lutherans to place over a child when it comes out of the font, that is, after it has been baptized. This ceremony is associated with the words, "As thou art now clothed with this pure, white, and unspotted garment, so mayest thou evermore be clothed with the innocence of Our Lord and Saviour Jesus Christ, for whose sake God has made thee His child and received thee as an heir of eternal life." [*]

The chrisom should be made of very fine linen, about 18″ by 33″ with a ½″ hem all around. A large cross in outline stitch may decorate the center. Inside the cross the symbols of Holy Baptism may also be stitched in outline. The chrisom should be folded like the baptismal towel so that it may be conveniently placed over the child and removed again after the ceremony.

Silver Towels

Some altar guilds make special towels, called *silver towels,* for drying the sacred vessels after they are washed. These towels are made of soft linen, 18″ by 27″, with a narrow hem and a simple cross.

Dustcloths

While the church is being cleaned, *dustcloths* are sometimes put over the altar, paraments, and chancel furnishings. They may be made of

[*] *Pro Ecclesia Lutherana* (December 1936), p. 19. See also Friedrich Lochner, *Liturgische Formulare für etliche Handlungen und Acte, nebst Gebeten, Collecten und einem Anhang* (St. Louis: Concordia Publishing House, 1895), pp. 193, 194.

cotton. The size will depend on the object to be covered. A simple cross should be sewed in the center of each cloth to show its sacred use. Dust-cloths are to be used only when cleaning; at no other time should they cover the altar, pulpit, and lectern.

Vesting the Altar

To vest the altar, first place a cere linen on the mensa. Then attach the proper frontal. Over the frontal hang the superfrontal, with the cloth to which it is attached extending over the mensa and held in place with a heavy flat rod in back. Place the protector linen on the mensa and over it the fair linen. Make sure that the fair linen hangs down the same distance over each end of the altar.

Making the Sacred Linens

The sacred linens are not as difficult to make as the paraments and vestments. Every altar guild can learn to sew and embroider them if the members are willing to work slowly, patiently, and carefully. Linen which is not preshrunk must be shrunk before it is sewn. Otherwise the pieces will not fit properly once they are laundered. Threads should be pulled for the proper size, and the linen then cut along the pulled threads. All the linens are sewn by hand. Machine work is not considered proper. The edges are hemmed, not hemstitched. The usual 20 stitches an inch applies to all linens. A 9 between sewing needle and No. 100 cotton thread should be used. All embroidery should be flat so as not to interfere with other objects or with proper handling.

It is no longer considered good taste to sew lace on church linens and vestments or to do any hemstitching. If lace is used, it must be real lace, such as Duchesse, Brussels, Rose Point, but never crocheted lace.

Laundering the Linens

Linens such as purificators and towels should be laundered after each use, and fair linens, surplices, and the like should be washed and ironed at least once a month. If the linens are taken home for laundering, they should not be washed with the family laundry. If possible, all church laundry should be done in a working sacristy or parish house. A special utensil should be provided and reserved for the purpose.

For good results, put linens in cold water and let them stand for a while; then add mild soap and bring the water slowly to a boil. At the boiling point the heat should be turned off and the linens allowed to stand for a few minutes. They should then be squeezed between the hands to rid them of as much soap as possible. They should be rinsed several times in clear water.

Do not use any starch or blueing.

Then wrap the linens in a turkish towel. After they have been in the towel for at least 30 minutes, they should be ironed, first on the wrong side and then on the right, so that both sides of the hems are perfectly dry.

The chalice pall with the aluminum plates inside may be laundered with the rest of the linens. But before it is taken out of the water, it should be brushed with a soft brush on both sides. Then it should be rinsed and dried in a turkish towel and ironed smooth.

Fair linens and protector linens cannot usually be stored flat in a drawer. They may be folded end to the center as when they are taken off the altar, or they may be rolled on newspaper or cardboard rollers covered with white paper. The linens must be perfectly dry before they are rolled, or they may ripple and later lie unevenly on the mensa.

Corporals should be folded in nine squares wrong side out so that they will unfold right side up on the altar. Purificators should be folded in nine squares with the cross right side up when finished. Baptismal and lavabo towels are also folded right side up.

It is necessary to inspect the fair linen on the altar at least once a week. If it is at all wrinkled or soiled, it should be replaced with a clean one.

Linens will remain white longer when stored between blue rather than white tissue paper. If the linens are hung in the sun to dry, the sun will bleach them white.

Purificators stained with wine or lipstick should be soaked in warm water for a long time and then rubbed thoroughly till the stain has faded out.

Wax drippings may be removed either by soaking the linen in cold water and then brushing off the hardened wax or by placing some absorbent paper underneath and ironing the linen carefully with a hot iron. Black wax spots, left by drippings from a candle snuffer, are very difficult to remove. Therefore the candle snuffers should be kept clean at all times to prevent such spots.

CHAPTER XIV

About Vestments

Clerical

In the Old Testament God prescribed the vestments to be worn by the high priests, the priests, and the Levites in the performance of their duties (Ex. 28:1; 39:4). These vestments were, of course, abrogated with the coming of the New Testament. But the principle and need for clerical vestments caused the development in Christian liberty of traditional garments for clergymen also in the New Testament church. In the 16th-century Reformation the traditional garments were retained by Lutherans. Later their use was abandoned at times and in places, but they still belong to our Christian and Lutheran heritage. It is therefore fitting that the altar guild make a study of their history and use. It should learn to know them even though the clergymen in its particular church are prevented by circumstances from wearing some or all of them. The present liturgical movement, which is affecting all Christian churches, is helping to restore many of the historical clerical vestments to those churches which once discarded them.

The Cassock

The cassock was once, and in principle still is, the everyday dress of a Christian clergyman. Therefore it is really not a vestment if we define vestments as garments worn only for divine worship. It is more precisely a garment over which a clergyman wears his vestments. It is black in color and should be made of wool serge or of cooler materials for warmer climates. It is fitted to the upper part of the body and extends into a full and flowing skirt from waist to ankles. At the neck it has a narrow band which fits around a white clerical collar. The neckband has a small step, or opening, in front. One style is single-breasted and buttons all the way down the front. Another style is double-breasted with fastenings, perhaps snaps, from collar to waist.

For convenience in adjusting the length and for the sake of appearance a cincture is usually worn around the waist. The cincture is usually of the same material as the cassock, 3″ to 4″ wide, 9′ to 12′ long, with or without fringe on the ends.

The Gown

The black clergy gown is also not really a vestment or a specifically clerical garment. It was the ordinary street garb of professors, judges, public officials, and clergymen in the 16th century. At that time the garment had a yoke fitted over the shoulders, and from the yoke the

Cassock

Gown with bands, or tabs

material hung down to the ankles in full folds. It had wide sleeves and a simple collar. The gowns manufactured in our day are of many different cuts and styles, but most of them are of the academic variety. In some European countries during the last 200 years a combination cassock and gown developed and was worn with a *ruffled collar*. It became popular in Norway and Denmark and is also sometimes seen in our country. Instead of the ruffled collar, *bands (Beffchen)* came to be worn with the black gown. These have no symbolic or ecclesiastical significance for Lutherans. They are simply a part of a gown worn by secular officials as well as clergymen in various countries including our own.

A *tippet*, or scarf, was added to the black gown in England and elsewhere. In Norway the scarf took the shape of a narrow tasseled, black silk stole over a black gown in the manner of some American clergymen. The *chaplain's scarf* of the American and the British armed forces is a kind of Norwegian black stole, but again it is not an ecclesiastical vestment. It is a chaplain's scarf, an item of uniform.

A *square cap, biretta,* or *skullcap* is used as a head covering with the cassock and black gown. A modern hat or cap is not suitable. A variety of caps and birettas may be obtained from good ecclesiastical supply houses.

When another garment is needed over the cassock or gown in cold and inclement weather, a black *cape* may be used outdoors. This is a sleeveless overcoat which is closed at the front over the chest with a morse, or clasp.

The Surplice

The white linen *surplice* is a vestment worn over a cassock by clergymen and certain laymen in the performance of the divine services in general. It originated as a substitute for the alb in cold churches of northern Europe. The alb, which fits the body snugly and has narrow sleeves, could not be put on over a thick woolen, fur-lined cassock. Therefore the surplice was designed to go on over a fur coat.

The beauty and dignity of the surplice lies in its fullness and length. If it is cut generously and falls to the ankles or at least within 6″ from the floor, it is far more graceful than a shorter one. It is also less likely to wrinkle when the wearer sits. The sleeves may be so full and wide that the bottoms fall to the ankle, and the tops should be at least long enough to fall to the wrists. The yoke should be oval and not square, the material gathered or smocked at the yoke. The surplice should always be made of linen or Dacron/cotton and not of rayon or other materials. Wrinkle-resistant linen is now available and is most suitable for surplices. If the altar guild wants to make surplices and other vestments, it should secure patterns from a reputable firm. Sometimes a white Latin cross is embroidered on the front of the surplice about 2″ below the yoke. Apparels in the color of the church year may be attached with snaps on the front bottom hem of the surplice (as on alb, p. 89).

The use of surplices is not restricted to clergymen. They may be worn also by lay assistants, servers, choristers, and acolytes.

A vestment similar to the surplice is the *sleeveless rochet*. It gives the

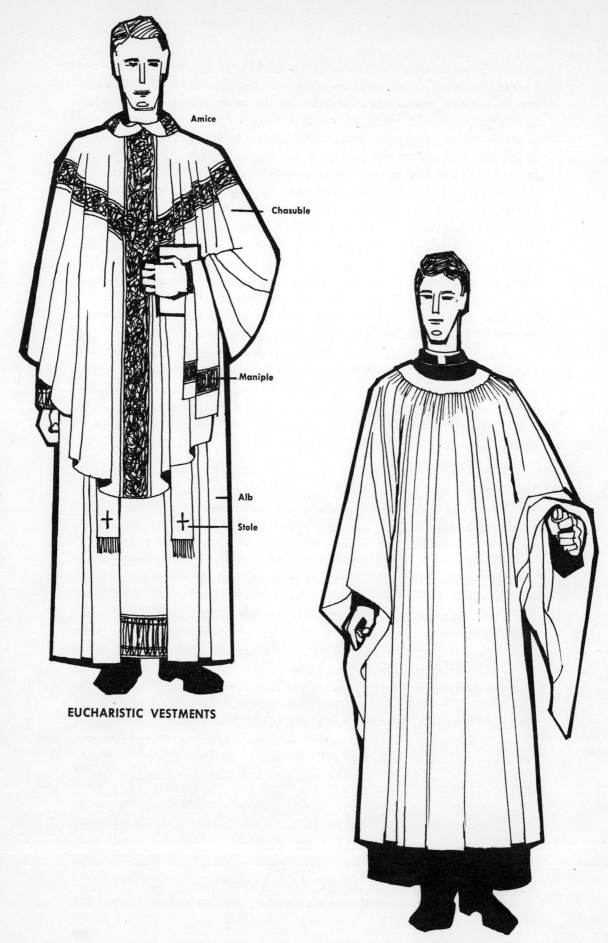

Amice

Chasuble

Maniple

Alb

Stole

EUCHARISTIC VESTMENTS

SURPLICE

wearer more freedom in the use of his arms than does the surplice. In Lutheran tradition it is very long, falling to the ankles. It may be made like the surplice, except that the sleeves are omitted and the sides may be left open. For the cotta see p. 92.

In recent years, white clergy gowns have been introduced in a few places for summer use. They are of the same material and shape as the black gown. This innovation is unfortunate, since such a garment is not a vestment and has no ecclesiastical significance. It is also unnecessary, because a full-length surplice or alb, which can be worn without a cassock or gown underneath, is even cooler than a white gown. When an alb or surplice is worn in this way, however, it should be used with a black shirt or vest and a clerical collar.

In laundering the white linen vestments, the altar guild should remember that blueing and starch are not to be used.

The Eucharistic Vestments

The Eucharistic vestments are, in the order in which the celebrant puts them on over the cassock, the amice, the alb, the cincture, the maniple, the stole, and the chasuble. All or some of these may be worn by Lutheran pastors in the celebration of the Holy Communion service. For this reason we give a brief description of each of them.

The Amice

The *amice* is the neckcloth anciently used with the alb and other garments. It is a rectangular piece of linen about 22″ by 30″ or larger with a ½″ hem all around. Shoulder tapes 72″ long are sewed to each end of the upper long edge. In the center of the upper portion about 2″ below the hem a simple cross is embroidered. To the upper edge and also centered is sewed a silk damask apparel about 3″ by 18″ or larger, which may be changed according to the colors of the church year. The amice is put on by folding back the appareled edge, laying it on the head as a modern nurse dons her head covering, and tying it in place with the tapes across the breast and around the waist. After all the vestments have been put on, the amice is pushed back so that the apparel will form a collar about the neck and resting on the shoulder. The traditional prayer which is said when the amice is put on refers to it as the "helmet of salvation" (Eph. 6:17). It probably acquired this symbolical meaning because it was first placed on the head before being laid back as a collar.[1]

The Alb

The *alb* is the earlier white linen vestment from which the surplice and rochet later developed. It covers the cassock completely. The sleeves are narrow, and the upper part fits the shoulders and body quite closely, but the lower part is cut generously so that it has a beautiful flowing appearance. It is slit about 12″ down the front so that it may slip over the head in vesting and then be closed with buttons. At the front and

[1] For pictures of the amice and how it is to be put on, see Herbert Norris, *Church Vestments: Their Origin and Development* (London: J. M. Dent & Sons, 1949), pp. 84—87; or the American ed. (New York: E. P. Dutton & Co. Inc., 1950), pp. 84—87.

back of the skirt near the edge, silk damask or brocade apparels about 7" by 14" may be attached; just above the wrists on the sleeves, apparels about 3" by 8". The alb symbolizes innocence and the robe of righteousness which is ours as Christians.

The Maniple

The *maniple* is purely a ceremonial vestment worn over the left arm near the wrist. It is made of silk damask, usually follows the colors of the church year, and has a 1" fringe at each end. The maniple should be about 2½" wide and 44" long. Whenever the celebrant is also the preacher, the maniple and chasuble may be removed before the sermon and put on again before the Offertory.

The Stole

The *stole* is a band of silk or silk damask about 2" wide at the center and gradually increasing to about 5" wide at the ends. The overall length is about 9'. The reason for making the stole so long is so that it will extend below the chasuble after it has been crossed over the breast and fastened with the cincture whenever full Eucharistic vestments are worn. The stole represents the yoke of Christ. A clergyman wears a stole around his neck for sacramental and some other services. No unordained person should wear a stole. One stole should be provided for each liturgical color.

The easiest way for an altar guild to make a stole is to buy a cutout kit. Such kits, available from reputable firms, contain all materials needed for making a stole, precut and ready for embroidery and assembly. The end of the stole may be decorated with a cross or a suitable symbol for the color of the season and finished with a 2" fringe. The stole may also be decorated with a running design from the ends partway or all the way to the center. The use of symbols all by themselves can be overdone. It is important to use well-chosen decorative designs to enhance the meaning and beauty of the symbols, for particularly against a very plain background the symbols by themselves may seem too stark. A stole may also be left entirely without decoration, except that it should have a small cross in the center to indicate its sacred use.

When and for what purposes the stole should be used according to Lutheran tradition is a matter that concerns the wearer more than the altar guild and need not be discussed here. If the altar guild is charged with the duty of laying out the stole for other than the celebration of the Holy Eucharist, it should ask the pastor for detailed instructions.

The stole symbolizes our Lord's perfect obedience by which He obtained for us the stole or robe of eternal life. This is indicated in the prayer which the minister may say as he puts it on: "Give me again, O Lord, the stole of immortality which I lost in the transgression of my first parents, and though I am unworthy to come to Thy sacred mystery, grant that I may rejoice in the same everlastingly."

The Chasuble

The *chasuble* is the principal Eucharistic vestment. The name comes from the Latin *casula*, which means a hut or little house, for the garment covered the whole body and even served as a kind of portable house for those traveling.[2] It was made of a semicircle of cloth with a neckhole for the head and neck to pass through, and when it was put on, it hung down to the feet. To free the arms and hands, the material had to be gathered in folds on the forearm, leaving the front and back draped. Later the sides were cut shorter, making the shape elliptical and reducing the material that had to be lifted on the arms. In the course of time, many other shapes were produced for reasons of convenience, taste, and different kinds of materials and ornamentations that were used. However, its development need not be discussed in detail here.

The elliptical shape is still the most desirable today. The front should be 40″ or longer. The back may be 45″ or more; the sides, 25″ or more. Fullness of cut and graceful folds give the chasuble greater dignity and beauty. It may be made of white linen or colored silk or damask in the colors of the church year. It need not be ornamented at all, but it is usually decorated with a straight orphrey down the front and a cross in the shape of a Y in the back. The arms of the cross extend up to the shoulder to make the Y cross. The straight orphrey down the front is called the pillar.

If the chasuble is made of white linen, the Y cross and the pillar may be simply outlined in chain stitch or made of strips of linen first embroidered and then appliqued before the chasuble is sewed together at the shoulders.

A chasuble made of silk damask may have orphreys of strips of silk, velvet, tapestry, cloth of gold, or 3″ to 4″ galloons made for the purpose. These materials should be embroidered before they are appliqued. The center of the Y cross may be ornamented with a symbol or monogram of Christ. The cross may also take the shape of a Latin cross instead of a Y cross.

To add beauty to the chasuble, it may be lined with silk or satin of a contrasting color. An inner lining, however, is not desirable, because the garment should fall in soft and graceful folds from the shoulders and over the arms.

When the celebrant puts on the chasuble, he may pray: "O Lord, who hast said, My yoke is easy and My burden is light, grant that I may so be able to bear it as to attain Thy grace." This prayer indicates the symbolism of the chasuble and signifies that the wearer is in the service of Jesus Christ, doing His will and working according to His directions.

The Dalmatic and Tunicle

When the celebrant is assisted by an ordained deacon and subdeacon, the deacon may wear a *dalmatic* and the subdeacon a *tunicle*. Other assisting clergymen may also wear a tunicle. The dalmatic and the tunicle are very much alike; both are often called either dalmatic or tunicle. The dalmatic, however, is ornamented more elaborately than the tunicle. These garments are made of the same material as the chasuble. They are long robes with sleeves, similar to the alb, but without any fullness. At the

[2] St. Isidore of Seville, writing about 600: "The casula is a garment furnished with a hood; and is a diminutive of 'casa,' a cottage, seeing that, like a small cottage or hut, it covers the entire person." Quoted by Norris, p. 61.

91

bottom they are about 40″ from side to side, and the length is about 45″. They are decorated with orphreys from the neck to the bottom. The sides are open 20″ or more from the bottom.

These vestments symbolize joy and gladness. The ancient prayer for putting on the dalmatic is "Clothe me, O Lord, with the robe of salvation and the garment of gladness, and ever set about me the dalmatic of justice."

The Miter and Pectoral Cross

Some Lutheran churches in Europe have bishops; in America, too, we have officials who exercise the office of a bishop even though they do not hold the title. Therefore we should mention the *miter* and *pectoral cross*.

The miter is the head covering of a bishop. It is made of damask and has the shape of a triangle in front and back. Ribbon pendants are attached to the back.

The pectoral cross is a distinctive ornament of bishops as part of their vestments. Therefore crosses and crucifixes of any size should not be worn with gowns or albs or surplices by clergymen who are not entitled to that distinction. It has been suggested that if they must wear a cross, they should put it underneath the outer garment so that they may still have the comfort of it without creating a false impression by displaying it publicly.

OTHER VESTMENTS

The Cope

The *cope* is a cloak or cape open in front, fastened there with a clasp or piece of material called a *morse*, and furnished in back with a cowl, or hood. It is used for ceremonial occasions other than the Holy Eucharist, such as processions (also at the Holy Communion service), ordination and installation rites, confirmation, the morning service without Holy Communion, matins and vespers on feast days, and the like. It is not exclusively a clerical vestment and may be worn by laymen as well as by clergy as a vestment of dignity.

The effectiveness of a cope depends on the gracefulness of its folds and the beauty of its material rather than on elaborate embroidery and other rich ornamentation. It is made of silk damask in the colors of the church year. The shape is an almost perfect semicircle. An orphrey as wide as 6″ may cover the length of the straight edge. The orphrey may be cloth of gold or some other contrasting color. The cope should be made long enough to hang to the feet.

Many copes today have only an imitation hood in the form of a shield, which is nothing more than an excuse for embroidery and other ornamentation. Instead of such a shield, why not a real hood made of the same material as the cope? When the hood is properly attached to the back, it will hang gracefully and may itself have a tassel or other ornamentation.

For Acolytes or Altar Boys

Acolytes and altar boys are properly vested in cassock and surplice or cotta. The black cassock is better than a colored one. It may be made

Cope

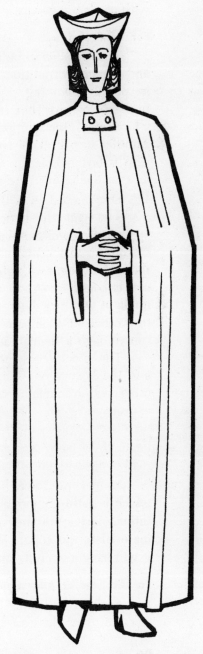

Women's choir and confirmation vestment

of heavy cotton material. The surplice or cotta may be white linen or cotton. It should hang below the knees and may be ankle length. A cotta is similar to a surplice, except that it is not gathered at the yoke, which may be square instead of round, and the sleeves need be only elbow length.

For the Choir

Choir members may wear a black cassock and white surplice. The surplice is more graceful if it falls below the knees. Although the surplice was originally a garment for males alone, it is now worn also by female choir members. Academic gowns are not churchly and should be avoided in vesting the choir. Women choristers should have their heads covered. Churchly caps, such as a small coif, a Canterbury cap, or a simple black toque, are suitable. Oxford caps are not desirable, for they are associated with academic gowns.

For Confirmation

That persons to be baptized or confirmed dress in white is an ancient and symbolic tradition. The white dress, however, is not traditionally a special gown but a white everyday dress. The custom presents no problem for girls, but it does for boys, since they do not ordinarily wear white suits. One solution to the problem is to rent white suits for the boys. Another is to provide special confirmation gowns for both boys and girls. This is being done, but unfortunately the gowns are usually of academic design. Such gowns are most unsuitable for the solemn rite of confirmation.

Our suggestion is that a white capelike garment be used. It may be made of white linen or cotton and in such a way that it will be very appropriate confirmation dress for both boys and girls. Since it is a Biblical custom for women to have their heads covered in church, it is fitting that the custom begin with girls at the time of their confirmation. A *confirmation veil* is considered most appropriate for the solemn occasion. The veil is made of very fine linen, 27" to 30" square, with a 2" hem. It is fastened to the hair at each side with pins or with an 8" length of elastic or tape run through a hem under the hair.

CHAPTER XV

About the Use of Lights in the Church

We are not concerned about the utilitarian use of lights in the church, but only the symbolical and ceremonial use. This symbolical and ceremonial use goes back to the Old Testament, where the symbolism of light is referred to often and the ceremonial use was prescribed by God Himself for the church's worship.

Light and the things related to it, such as fire and burning incense, are symbols of God, sacrifice, and prayer. If they are used properly, they may enhance the liturgy.

"God is light, and in Him is no darkness at all" (1 John 1:5). He created light. He went before the Children of Israel as a pillar of light. In a special sense Christ is "Light of light" (Nicene Creed). He is "the true light, which lighteth every man that cometh into the world" (John 1:9). In the vision of the heavenly Jerusalem, "the Lamb is the light [lamp] thereof" (Rev. 21:23). Light is symbolical of God.

Fire symbolizes sacrificial love. Oil burning in a lamp and burning candles are symbols of sacrificial love, both of Christ and of His disciples. "Be ye therefore followers of God, as dear children, and walk in love, as Christ also hath loved us and hath given Himself for us an offering and a sacrifice to God for a sweet-smelling savor." (Eph. 5:1, 2)

Incense is a symbol of prayer. "Let my prayer be set forth before Thee as incense" (Ps. 141:2). In the heavenly vision, "another angel came and stood at the altar, having a golden censer, and there was given unto him much incense, that he should offer it with the prayers of all saints upon the golden altar which was before the throne. And the smoke of the incense, which came with the prayers of the saints, ascended up before God out of the angel's hand." (Rev. 8:3, 4)

Quality of Lights

Candles used for symbolical and ceremonial purposes are traditionally made of beeswax or at least 51 percent beeswax. If necessary, candles made of inferior materials may be used in less important positions. However, it is desirable that at least the Eucharistic candles and the Paschal candle be of beeswax. Unbleached or brown candles may be used at Tenebrae, Good Friday, and funerals. Otherwise they should be white and never colored, not even for the Advent wreath if it is placed in the chancel. Metal or cardboard tubes painted to resemble candles, with inner springs attached to push up small candles, or any device for the use of gas or electric lights are not considered in harmony with the genuine character of divine worship.

Number of Lights

For the celebration of the Holy Communion service, at least two candles generally stand on the altar. Since these were the only candles used at a low celebration and stood on the extreme ends of the altar on either side of the crucifix, these two candles have come to be called *Eucharistic lights*. But according to tradition, the number of single candles on the altar for the Holy Eucharist may vary from two to seven and even eight, and a celebration may be held with only one. For practical purposes, however, it may be well to designate only two candles as Eucharistic lights. Traditionally candelabra with three, five, or seven candles are not regarded as Eucharistic lights. But since these are often used on the altar together with the single end-candles, a distinction should be made. Confusion may be avoided by calling all other candles on the altar, even the single candles, *office lights*.

One or more candles are used for all divine services. The number of candles may be regulated by the type of service held and the character of the day or season. Minor services will naturally not have as many candles as the chief service, at least not on the same day or in the same season. High feasts and seasons will be distinguished from penitential days and seasons by employing more and fewer lights, respectively. The type of candlestick used may also vary. Brass or precious metal candlesticks may be used for high feasts and seasons and simple wooden ones for the penitential seasons, especially Lent, Passiontide, and Holy Week (except Maundy Thursday).

The number of candles on the altar will probably have to be limited to two candelabra and two Eucharistic lights. Two candles are sufficient. The historic Lutheran practice was to have only two. If more are used, they need not all be the same height, but may rise from one to the next towards the cross. Any other lights will have to be placed on the pavement or on wall brackets. Care should be exercised so that the use of lights is not overdone. Anything that borders on the theatrical or sentimental is certainly out of place in the house of God.

Acolyte Candlesticks

Candlesticks carried by acolytes may be 2½′ to 3½′ high, with knobs in the middle and a base at the bottom for standing on the floor. They may be made of any suitable material. Both hands are used in carrying them. When held abreast by two or more acolytes, each acolyte holds the knob with his outer hand and the base with his other. All are held at the same height.

Torches have no base and are placed in a rack when not in use. They are carried with one hand, the other laid flat on the breast. When carried by two abreast, they are held in the outer hands.

When candles are used outdoors, it is necessary to carry them in *lanterns* fixed to staves. The staves should be about 4′ high and carried with both hands.

Acolyte candles may be used for indoor and outdoor functions, litur-

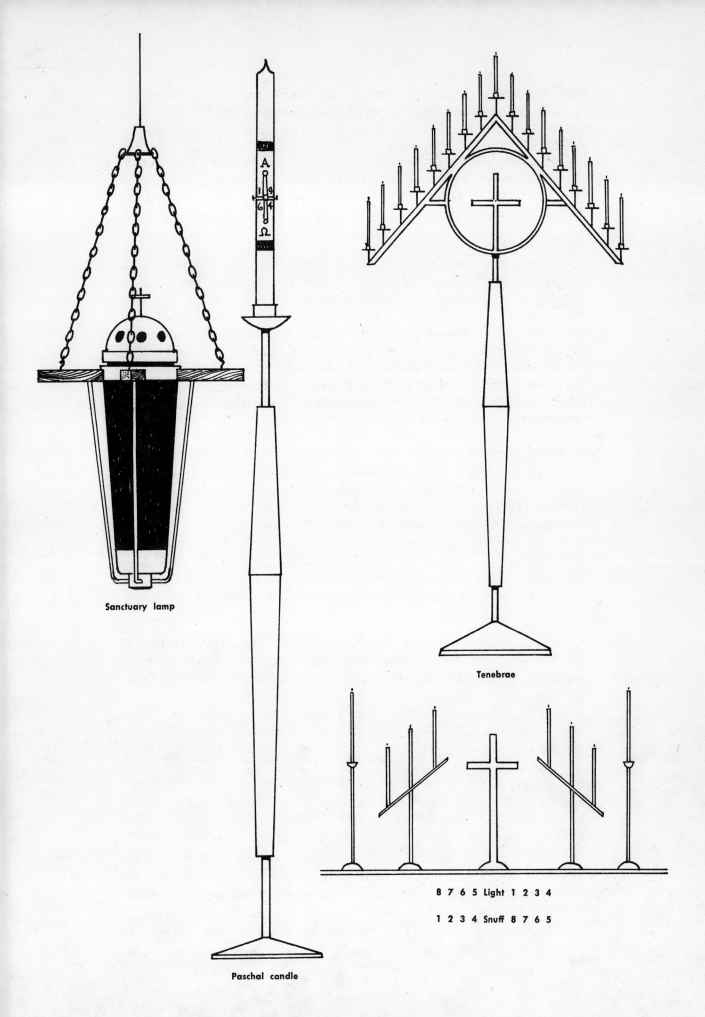

Sanctuary lamp

Paschal candle

Tenebrae

8 7 6 5 Light 1 2 3 4

1 2 3 4 Snuff 8 7 6 5

gical and nonliturgical. Sometimes they are used in processions of children or choirs going to and from the parish house and the church.

Sanctus Candle

In some churches a sanctus candle is lighted in the Holy Communion service from the singing of the Sanctus to the end of the Distribution. This candle is generally fixed to a bracket, or sconce, on the wall on the Epistle side of the altar. An acolyte or server lights and extinguishes it.

Sanctuary Lamps

Wherever the ancient practice of reserving the Blessed Sacrament for communicating the sick is observed, at least one sanctuary lamp is kept burning continuously near the place of reservation. Olive oil or vegetable oil is used in the lamp. The sanctuary lamp is usually suspended from the ceiling on the Gospel side of the chancel over or near the altar rail. It may also be placed on a metal stand or wall bracket. It should not be on the altar. The glass of the lamp should be untinted, for the light is to be white. Other lamps hung in the chancel may have colored glass and not burn continuously. If more than one is used, the lamps should be odd in number — three, five, or seven.

Baptismal Candles

Baptismal candles and font candles may be used at Holy Baptism. The baptismal candle may be lighted and given to the child after its baptism. The font candle may be carried by an acolyte to the font and held there during the service. Sometimes the two candles are identical. They are not carried in candleholders but held in the hand, sometimes with a baptismal napkin. A baptismal candle given to the child and lighted every year on the anniversary of its baptism can be a valuable aid in teaching the child the ongoing meaning of Holy Baptism throughout life.

Hand Candles

At the feast of the Presentation of Our Lord and the Purification of the Blessed Virgin Mary, February 2, called Candlemas, lighted hand candles may be held by members of the congregation. Because the Light of the world was brought into the temple on this day, candles are traditionally blessed immediately before the Holy Communion service and given to everyone present. When the candles are distributed, the Nunc Dimittis is sung with this antiphon repeated after each verse: "A Light to lighten the Gentiles and the Glory of Thy people Israel." This is followed by a procession in the church, during which lighted candles are carried and appropriate hymns and anthems are sung. Later, during the Holy Communion service, all the worshipers hold their lighted candles again when the Gospel is read and from the Consecration to the Distribution.

Hand candles may also be used in other services and ceremonies, especially in the Easter vigil. In the first part of this service, after the Paschal candle has been lighted and is moving in procession up the aisle, the light from the Paschal candle is gradually spread to hand candles held by the congregation. Thus the fact is proclaimed that the light of

Christ is meant for all Christians and that everyone must do his part in the evangelization of the world. While the people's candles are lighted, the deacon sings: "The light of Christ"; the people reply: "Thanks be to God."

A very simple way to make a shield for a hand candle so that it will not drip on the hand is to cut an X in the center of a piece of paper and push the candle through the X so that the paper rests on the hand.

The Paschal Candle

The Paschal candle is a symbol of our Lord's resurrection and His visible presence here on earth during the following 40 days. The candle is lighted from the new fire kindled at the beginning of the Easter vigil. Before lighting it the minister cuts a cross in the wax. Above the cross he inscribes A and below it Ω, the first and last letters of the Greek alphabet. These symbolize that Christ is the same yesterday, today, and forever. Then the numerals of the current year are inscribed between the arms of the cross to signify that the risen Christ shall be a "pillar of fire" also in this year to lead us to the heavenly promised land. In the center and in each end of the cross, wax nails are affixed to symbolize the five wounds of Christ.

After the Paschal candle has been brought into the chancel, it is placed in a stand on the pavement near the Gospel horn of the altar. It remains there and is lighted for all liturgical services till the reading of the Gospel of the feast of the Ascension. On that day it is extinguished by an acolyte when the words of the Gospel are proclaimed: "He was received up into heaven and sat on the right hand of God." (Mark 16:19)

Funeral Candlesticks

Funeral candlesticks may be set around the coffin after it has been placed at the head of the nave parallel to the center aisle for the funeral service. The candlesticks are about 4' high and may be of wood. The candles may be unbleached or brown. Seven candlesticks may be used, three on each side and one at the east end of the coffin. Only two on each side of the coffin may suffice; at times, only one on each side.

The Advent Wreath

The custom of lighting an Advent wreath during the four weeks before Christmas has become increasingly popular in recent years. The lighting of the candles symbolizes the age before the coming of Christ, when the light of prophecy concerning the Messiah became brighter and brighter till He Himself came and said: "I am the light of the world."

The wreath consists of evergreen branches tied to a metal or wooden hoop. To the hoop four candles are fixed at equal distances. The wreath may be suspended with violet ribbons from a stand made for it, from the ceiling, or from a light fixture, or it may be placed on a table. The candles are white if the wreath is used in church.

On the eve of the First Sunday in Advent and for all services throughout the week till the eve of the Second Sunday in Advent, one candle is lighted. The next week two are lighted, the third week three, and the fourth week all four, always beginning the week on the eve of the Sunday, that is, Saturday evening.

The wreath's position in the church should not be such that it obscures or distracts from the altar.

Lighting and Extinguishing Candles

The candles nearest the altar crucifix are lighted first, beginning on the Epistle side. Two persons, one on either side of the crucifix, should perform the duty when there are many candles. If only one acolyte does the work, he should light all the candles on the Epistle side first, then those on the Gospel side.

In extinguishing the candles, the reverse order is observed. Beginning on the Gospel side, the acolyte first puts out the candle farthest from the altar crucifix. After all the candles on the Gospel side have been extinguished, those on the Epistle side are put out in the same order.

The candles may be lighted during the organ prelude before the service and extinguished during the postlude after the service.

It is but seemly that the person who lights and extinguishes the candles be vested in cassock and surplice or cotta. He should light the candles with a taper and extinguish them with a snuffer. Combinations of the two are available. The handle should be long enough to reach the candles easily.

The Placing and Care of Candles

One of the duties of the altar guild members will be to place the candles where and when they are needed. For this reason they should ask the pastor what candles will be required. Candles should be wiped with a soft cloth after they have been placed and, at the same time, be made to stand straight. The wick should be inspected and trimmed if necessary for easy lighting. If a candle has become smudged, it can easily be cleaned with a cloth and a little turpentine.

It will not be necessary to replace candles until they have burned down so far that they will not last through the services for the day. To determine this, it should be observed how far they burn down in an hour. Most candles burn about an inch an hour under normal conditions.

The use of brass candle followers or savers should be avoided, especially on the altar. They make candles look unnatural and give a spotty appearance to the altar setting, which is not pleasing. If cheap candles which do not burn well without followers have to be used, they may be set in candlesticks that are not on the altar. The candles on the altar should be of such quality that they will burn evenly without artificial devices.

Candles improve in their burning quality with age. It is therefore wise to buy them well in advance of the time when they will be needed. They should be kept in the manufacturer's cartons and laid flat in a cool place. If they are not stored properly, they may warp or melt together from heat.

Newly placed candles should be burned a little before the service to make lighting by the acolytes easier and to discover any possible defects in the candlewicks.

Contemporary candlestick   Fritz Kühn

CHAPTER XVI

About the Church Year and Liturgical Colors

The precedent for the Christian church year was the church year which God appointed for His people Israel in the Old Testament. The Christian church year, however, was not appointed but developed gradually. How did it develop, and what is its meaning for us today?

It began with the celebration of our Lord's resurrection. This tremendous event became at once the center of the church's faith, life, and worship. Easter was celebrated every Sunday. Later the anniversary of the Resurrection was observed as an annual celebration, and around it the other parts of the church year began to grow. Fifty days after Easter, Pentecost was celebrated as the feast of the outpouring of the Holy Spirit. The whole period from Easter to Pentecost was regarded as a prolonged Easter feast. With Easter in the center, the church year developed in both directions. Maundy Thursday, Good Friday, and Holy Saturday were observed as solemn days of preparation for Easter. This period of preparation was gradually made longer until it began with Septuagesima.

During the first three centuries of the church, it seems that no other parts of the church year existed, except the keeping of certain anniversary days of martyrs. This was the church year; it seems to have begun with Septuagesima and to have ended on the day before Septuagesima.

By the fourth century the advent of Christ came to be celebrated as the center of a small section of the church year. This section came at the end of the church year and not, as now, at the beginning. It celebrated primarily the appearance of Christ, the Epiphany, and the promise of His Second Advent, rather than His birth or incarnation.

When the original idea of this section changed and the birth of Christ became its central celebration, it was regarded as the beginning and no longer as the end of the church year. Like Easter, Christmas developed a season of preparation and an extension. The season of preparation was the period of Advent, and the season of extension was the Epiphany period.

With the joining together of these two sections, the larger centering in Easter and the smaller in Christmas, the church year had completed its main structure. All that was added to this structure in later centuries were details and ornamentations. Days of apostles, martyrs, and saints, as well as commemorations of events in the history of the church, completed the church year as it has come down to us.

This is a very brief description of the development of the Christian church year, but it helps us to understand its structure and to correct current false ideas about it. The church year is one complete yearly cycle centering in Easter. This cycle contains two sections, the Easter section and the Christmas section. Both sections are built up in the same way. Both begin with a season of preparation, climax with the celebration of the central and related feasts, and end with a period of extension. Thus the Christmas section begins with Advent, centers in the feasts of Christmas and Epiphany, and closes with the extended Epiphany Sundays. The Easter section begins with Septuagesima, centers in the feasts of the Resurrection, Ascension, and Pentecost, and ends with the extension of the Sundays after Pentecost or Trinity.

What is the meaning of the church year for us today? The yearly cycles are not separated entities; they are like the circles of a spiral. They are yearly rounds of life lived in and with Christ and His church, leading us year after year upward and heavenward. Christ said: "I am come that they might have life and that they might have it more abundantly" (John 10:10). The church year may help us attain that life more abundantly.

The church year may also mean for us a way of devoting the time of our life to God, of sanctifying the time He grants us, of living it in union and communion with His body, the church.

The days are sanctified according to the Lutheran rite by the church's daily services of matins and vespers. The Lutheran reformers expected these to be conducted publicly in the parish churches every day. This custom fell into decline in the 18th and 19th centuries, but fortunately it is being restored more and more today. Even if not many parishioners can go to church daily for matins and vespers, they can be present in thought and spirit when they are conducted and in that way participate in the church's way of offering the day to God.

The week is hallowed in the church year by keeping the first day, Sunday, as the Lord's day. Each Sunday celebrates some phase of the mystery of our redemption. Therefore it has its own name and objective which should not be lightly disregarded or set aside for the observance of other things. The remembrance of our Lord's resurrection always dominates this first day of the week, fills it with joy, and makes the other days of the week attached to it days of grace. In Christian tradition the fourth and sixth days are station and fasting days, because our Lord's betrayal was negotiated on a Wednesday and He was crucified on a Friday. To keep station means to stand guard against temptation to sin, and to fast means to exercise self-denial and self-discipline as an act of faith and devotion.

The month is not regarded as a unit of time in the church year. The church-year units are the day, the week, and the year, except that the sacred seasons connected with the great feasts may be considered as units. But at the same time the rhythm of the natural year is not disregarded by the church year. This is true especially in regard to the natural seasons in the parts of the world where the church year originated. Easter coincides with spring, the end of the church year and its emphasis on the "last things" with fall and winter, and Christmas and Epiphany with the increase of light and lengthening daytime after the winter solstice. Another example is the observance of ember days, which is as old as the celebration of Christmas. The ember days are the Wednesday, Friday, and Saturday after December 13; the First Sunday in Lent; Whitsunday; and September 14. They refer to the quarters of the year in which the fruits of the earth are planted, grown, harvested, and stored. Allegorically the church refers this to the sowing and the resulting harvest of the seed of the Word, and from this interpretation comes the tradition of ordaining ministers as sowers of the Word on the ember days or in ember-day weeks.

The church year begins with Advent, a penitential season in preparation for Christmas, on the Sunday nearest St. Andrew's Day, November 30. While it is penitential, the season is not as solemn as Lent. The Third Sunday in Advent, called Gaudete, already anticipates the Christmas joy. However, it is a season of waiting for the promised Savior in His threefold advent: His advent in "the fullness of time," in Word and sacraments, and at the end of time.

Then the church celebrates Christmastide with three great feasts: Christ's nativity, His circumcision and the giving of the holy name of Jesus, and His epiphany by a star to the Magi and His baptism.

The first part of the church year centering in Christmas is then extended to join the part that centers in Easter. The extension is called the Epiphany season. In it the church celebrates additional epiphanies, or manifestations, of the deity of Him who was born of the Virgin Mary.

About 70 days before Easter, on Septuagesima Sunday, the church gets ready for the holy season of Lent, which begins Ash Wednesday. The name comes from the ceremony in which the church applies ashes to the foreheads of her people with the words: "Remember, O man, that thou art dust, and to dust shalt thou return." Lent consists of 40 fasting days. The Sundays in between are not *of* Lent but only *in* Lent. Lent ends with Passiontide, the second week before Easter, and Holy Week, the week before Easter. The last three days of Holy Week are Maundy Thursday, Good Friday, and Holy Saturday. The Tenebrae services are the matins of these three days, held on the previous evenings. Like Gaudete in Advent, the Fourth Sunday in Lent, Laetare, is a joyful Sunday. It anticipates the joy of Easter.

The church celebrates Eastertide with three great feasts over a period of 50 days. The first is that of the resurrection of our Lord, the second that of our Lord's ascension, and the third that of Pentecost. All three feasts are days of greatest joy, for He who was crucified, dead, and buried, arose again and ascended into heaven and sent the Holy Spirit, the Lord and Giver of Life.

The extension of Easter is the Pentecost, or Trinity season. In it the church celebrates from Sunday to Sunday the life-giving words and works of Christ till the church year ends.

Thus the whole year, all the time in the annual cycle, is hallowed by the church in grateful response to the redeeming grace of the Triune God. The church also remembers in grateful devotion to God the great apostles, martyrs, saints, and angels who were a part of her history. These commemorative days in the church calendar help us to translate the church's creed into the experiences of our own life in the realm of time.

The Church-Year Cycle

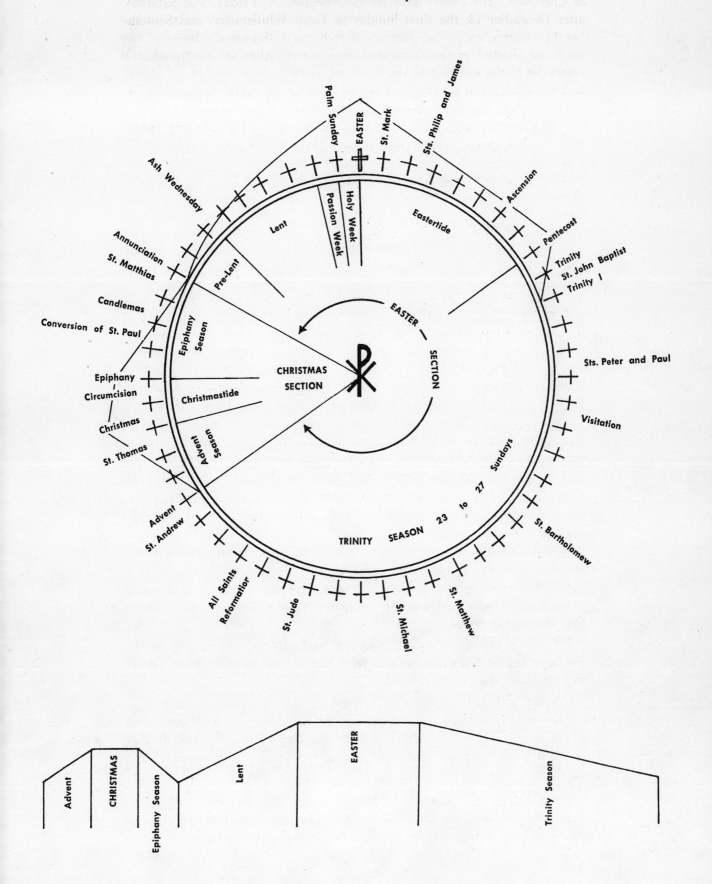

The Liturgical Colors

The Lutheran Church follows the late Western tradition of using five colors — white, red, green, violet, and black — to express the spirit of the days and seasons of the church year. Their significance is explained in the service book as follows:

White: Color of the Godhead, eternity, robe of the glorified Christ and the Angels, perfection, joy, purity.

Red: Color of fire, fervor, blood, martyrdom, love, victorious truth of Christian teaching based on the blood and righteousness of Christ.

Green: Color of abiding life, nourishment, rest; dominant color in nature.

Violet: Color of royal mourning and repentance.

Black: Absence of color, symbolical of death.[1]

Their Proper Use

White is used during Christmastide, that is, from and with vespers of Christmas Eve through the Epiphany octave, except for the saints' days. The use of white instead of green is permitted also from matins on January 14 to (but not at) vespers on the Saturday before Septuagesima Sunday. White is used during Eastertide, that is, from the eve of Easter to (but not at) matins of Rogation Monday, and from the eve of Ascension Day to (but not at) vespers on the eve of Pentecost. It is used on the Feast of the Holy Trinity and during its octave. It is used in the Holy Communion service on Maundy Thursday; on the festivals of the Presentation, Annunciation, Visitation, and Transfiguration; the Day of St. Michael and All Angels; the Conversion of St. Paul; the Nativity of St. John the Baptist; All Saints' Day; the dedication of a church and its anniversary; days of general or special thanksgiving; and on the festivals of saints not martyrs.

Red is used during Whitsuntide, that is, from and with vespers on the eve of Pentecost to vespers on the eve of Holy Trinity; on the Festival of the Reformation and during its octave; also for ordination and on all days of saints who died martyrs, except on Holy Innocents' Day when it falls during the week.

Green is used from and with matins on January 14 to vespers on the Saturday before Septuagesima and from the Second Sunday After Trinity to vespers on the eve of Advent.

Violet is used from and with vespers on the eve of Advent to vespers on the eve of Christmas, from vespers on the Saturday before Septuagesima to vespers on the eve of Easter, and for the Day of Humiliation. It may be used from and with matins on Rogation Monday to vespers on the Wednesday before Ascension Day, on ember days, and on Holy Innocents' Day when it falls during the week.

[1] *The Lutheran Liturgy* (St. Louis: Concordia Publishing House, 1955 and later printings), p. 425.

Black is used only on Good Friday.

The color of the day is not changed for the solemnization of holy matrimony or for the burial of the dead.[2]

Wall Calendars

The altar guild should provide the working sacristy and the homes of all its members with a church calendar which prescribes the details of the services and colors for each church year.[3]

[2] Ibid., pp. 425—427.

[3] We recommend the *Lutheran Liturgy* edition of the Lutheran Church Calendar, printed by the Ashby Company of Erie, Pa., and the Concordia Scripture Text Calendar. Both are sold by Concordia Publishing House, 3558 S. Jefferson Ave., St. Louis, Mo. 63118.

CHAPTER XVII

About the Use of Flowers in Church

"The glory of Lebanon shall come unto thee, the fir tree, the pine tree, and the box together, to beautify the place of My sanctuary; and I will make the place of My feet glorious" (Is. 60:13). This prophecy indicates the purpose of greenery and floral decorations in church. They are to beautify and make glorious the house of God where He is present with His people as they are gathered together in His name. Flowers are placed in church to worship and glorify God. They are an expression of the beauty and goodness of God. They symbolize spiritual joy and devotion. Properly used, flowers are an expression of our high regard and reverence for God and His house.

General Principles

Church decorations should have a unity of plan, be centered in a single object and harmonize with it in all parts. Therefore, before arranging and placing flower decorations in the chancel, the altar guild should consider the total picture. The center of the chancel is the altar. The eye should be led to it. This being so, the flower decorations placed in the chancel should be arranged in such a manner as to reach their climax on the altar. They should also harmonize with the chancel in all respects. This includes the architecture, size, furnishings, light, color, and other factors. If the flowers are kept in good harmony with their surroundings, they will enhance the beauty of the chancel and contribute to the dignity and impressiveness of the worship service.

Flower decorations should help to express the mood of the service of the day. If the mood is quiet and restrained, the flowers should be darker and less colorful. As the mood increases in joyfulness and festivity, the brighter and more numerous the flowers may be! But the number of flowers is not what counts. Their effectiveness depends not so much on their abundance as on their careful use. It is better to err on the side of simplicity than to overdecorate.

There are certain restrictions in the use of flowers in church which should not be taller than the arms of the altar crucifix. They should any part of it, nor should they ever be placed behind the crucifix. They should not be taller than the altar crucifix or the candles. They should not stand on the mensa of the altar, but on the gradine. If the altar has no gradine, the flowers should be placed in churchly floor standards beside the altar or on a shelf or other suitable platform. They should not obstruct any other significant decorations, such as carvings, pictures, and stained glass. Neither should they interfere with the movement of the officiants in conducting divine services. Potted plants are not seemly on the altar; they may be placed on the pavement around the altar. Ribbon bows and gaudy metallic paper should be removed from potted plants. Artificial flowers or tinted flowers should not be used, for only genuine things are in harmony with the church's worship. Flowers should not be placed in or on objects of a sacred character, such as the baptismal font, the chancel rail, a Bible, or a service book. They should not stand at the ends of the altar gradine but between the candlesticks and the altar crucifix. They should not be left in the church when they are wilted.

Flower Arrangement

Arranging flowers for church decorations and arranging them for display at home require somewhat different skills. Flower arrangements in the home are seen from closeup, but flowers in church are seen from a distance. In the home the color and design may be subtle, but in church the design must be clear-cut and bold.

Three types of arrangement are generally used for church decorations: the triangle design, the oval design, and the vertical design. The triangle design has a tall center stalk for the primary line and two horizontal stalks to each side for the secondary line. The other flowers are filled in around this design, producing both in shape and in color emphasis a triangle effect.

The oval design is made with lower center stalks around which the other stalks radiate, some of which are turned to the sides all around. This design is especially suitable in churches that have round arches.

The vertical design has a long vertical stalk in the center with the other stalks placed vertically around it and standing up harmoniously with it. This design is very effective where the vertical line in the church needs to be emphasized.

Color

The problem of color in flower arrangement for the church is also somewhat different than for the home. The color of the flowers in church should always be in harmony with the color of the church year used on a particular day. This does not mean that the flowers must all be the same color as the paraments, but there should be a harmony of color and an expression of the same symbolism and mood as the color of the church year.

Furthermore, the mood of the church year is at times such that no flowers at all are suitable. For example, no flowers are used in Advent and Lent, except that there may be flowers on Gaudete, the Third Sunday in Advent, and on Laetare, the Fourth Sunday in Lent. Also on days of penitence and prayer, flowers are omitted. In the Epiphany and Trinity seasons, some Sundays call for sparing use of flowers, while others demand more profuse use. The same thing applies to saints' days and other minor festivals. The spirit of feast days is best expressed with many flowers of colors which are particularly bright and joyful.

Flower Vases

Since flower vases on the altar are closely related to the altar crucifix and candlesticks, they should harmonize with them in design and material. Brass candlesticks and silver vases, for instance, would not be in good harmony. On the other hand, crystal vases harmonize with all metals and all flowers.

Oriental vases with decorations of non-Christian religions are not suitable. Neither are vases of a distinctly domestic character. Whether they are of metal or glass, they should be of a design both beautiful and ecclesiastical. When two or more vases are used on the altar, they should be identical. Vases used elsewhere in the chancel may be of a different shape and material, but all should be churchly in character.

The size of the vases will depend on the places where they are employed. Altar vases will be smaller than vases placed on floor standards at the sides of the altar. Much also depends on the size of the altar and the chancel. It is all a matter of good scale and proportions.

Easter Decorations

Since Easter is the central and highest feast of the entire church year, it calls for the greatest expression of adoration, gratitude, triumph, joy, and gladness also in the use of floral decorations. Then flowers can be employed in greater profusion than at any other time. Their very number should create the effect of shouting "Alleluia!"

It is not the number of flowers alone, however, that will produce the desired effect. What is more important than their number is the kinds of flowers and how they are used.

White flowers are the most significant for Easter and all white, at least for the Easter octave, are better than a mixture of colors. Since gold is a substitute for white, gold flowers may also be used, but for the octave itself, white are preferable. The Easter lily is the queen of the Easter flowers. Other white lilies, such as the calla lily, may be placed around the altar, but if possible, Easter lilies should be on the altar. Potted plants should be cut and put into vases. It will be necessary to put more than one stem in each vase; since Easter lilies do not show up well from a distance, the effect will not be festive unless the flowers are bunched. Two well-filled vases, one on each side of the crucifix, will be more effective than four or six with only a few lilies in each.

All the flowers should be arranged to guide eyes beyond themselves to the altar and the crucifix. The lilies on the altar should lead the eyes to the crucifix and all the flowers around the altar should be placed to lift eyes upward to the altar or in some way to emphasize it. They should also create a massive effect. Extreme care should be exercised that they do not look scattered and disorganized.

As a background to the white flowers, the east wall of the chancel on each side of the altar may be banked with green branches. Palm branches with their symbolism of victory are especially suitable. What could be more meaningful for Easter than a combination of lilies and palm branches? Many other green branches can also be used for the background. What is most important is that the overall floral decoration is well planned and executed, so that it will express the great joy of the Easter greeting, "The Lord is risen! He is risen indeed!"

Christmas Decorations

Next to Easter, Christmas is the most joyful feast of the Church. In the expression of Christmas joy, light plays an important part, for Christmas means that Christ, the Light, has come. The idea of light cannot very well be expressed with electric lights. For this purpose candles and flowers are needed. In many churches the regular electric lights are not used at all then, and only candles are lighted, especially for the midnight Eucharist. Candles are placed not only in the chancel but in the windows of the nave, on pew ends and pillars, and in the choir loft. Such "living light" at Christmas is very effective.

Greenery and flowers will also help to express the joy of Christmas. Among the greens, fir trees, fir branches, and holly are the most traditional. Plain fir trees placed against the east chancel wall on both sides of the altar are a basic decoration for Christmas. In addition to these, one or two decorated trees in the chancel, if there is room, or at the head of the nave will emphasize the spirit associated with the Christmas tree. Holly branches are especially good for decorating the windows and pillars.

The main emphasis must remain on the altar. White flowers are the most desirable on the altar during the Christmas octave. A beautiful effect may be created with white poinsettias on the altar and red poinsettias massed on the floor at both ends of the altar. Those placed on the altar should be cut and arranged in vases.

A Christmas crib, creche, or manger may form an important part of the Christmas decorations. It should include the figures of the Virgin Mary, Joseph, the Holy Babe, an ox, and an ass. Shepherds and sheep may be added to the scene for Christmas and later replaced by the Wise Men for Epiphany. The Nativity scene may be placed anywhere except in front of the altar. If it is large enough, the most effective place is on the Epistle side of the altar against a background of plain Christmas trees and near the chancel rail.

Decorations for a Wedding

A church wedding is a church service and should always be reverent, dignified, and worshipful. As in all church services, the focal point and center of worship is the altar.

Therefore also for weddings the church decorations should lead all eyes to the altar. This means that the altar flowers should receive primary consideration. Let them be the most beautiful and attractive of all. The color of the flowers will depend on the paraments and the color scheme chosen for the wedding. The paraments will be those current in the church year. They are not changed for a wedding.

The center aisle and the chancel entrance may also be decorated with flowers. The flowers along the aisle may be attached to the pew ends, either on standards or in hanging vases. The chancel entrance may be banked with flowers, or two large bouquets just inside the chancel, one on each side of the aisle, may be sufficient. .

Policy for Decorating

It is wise for the church to establish a firm policy as to who may decorate the chancel. Ordinarily the altar guild should be in sole charge and do all the work. Regardless of who furnishes the flowers, the arranging and placing of them is done by the altar guild. Everyone should also understand that the flowers must be brought at the time and to the place designated by the altar guild. All decorating must be completed at least 30 minutes before the beginning of any church service.

These rules and regulations apply also to weddings. When a florist is engaged to furnish the decorations and do the work, he should do it under the supervision of a member of the altar guild. The florist should be asked beforehand to respect the sacredness of the house of God and to do his work reverently.

Sending Flowers to the Sick

It is a beautiful custom to send the flowers which were used in church, especially the altar flowers, to members of the congregation who are ill. A card may be enclosed with a message like the following: "These flowers, used in our worship service this morning, are sent to you to assure you of the prayers of the congregation and to wish you our Lord's blessings. May they convey to you the peace and joy of God's house."

Flowers may be taller or shorter than the altar candles but not taller than the arms of the altar crucifix.

Some churches allow foliage arrangements instead of flowers during Advent and Lent. Examples: Advent wreath, Palm Sunday tree branches.

CHAPTER XVIII

About Christian Symbols

We shall mention in this chapter only some of the most commonly used symbols, primarily those employed in church embroidery. If the altar guild wishes to make a study of Christian symbolism or to use symbols extensively in embroidery, it should acquire some of the fine books which have been written on the subject.[1]

The cross is the symbol of our holy Christian faith and of our redemption. The decorative cross has many forms.

The *Latin Cross* (1) has the shape of the instrument of death on which our Savior died. In designing the cross, it is necessary to get good proportions. Very often it is made too thick and clumsy. One way to get satisfactory proportions is to cut twelve equal squares out of paper and arrange these in the form of a cross, eight squares high and five squares wide. Even these proportions, however, are clumsy when used in embroidery. There the cross must be made considerably more slender.

A word of caution is in place here concerning the multiplication of crosses. While every building, piece of furniture, vessel, vestment, parament, and linen used in divine worship is properly marked somewhere with a cross, crosses should not be multiplied to such an extent as to cheapen this sacred symbol. Neither should the holy cross be placed just anywhere; for example, on a floor where it would be stepped on or where it would be handled in a way that seems irreverent.

The *Greek Cross* (2) has four arms of equal length. *St. Andrew's Cross* (3) also has four arms of equal length, but stands on two ends like an X. It is also called the *Cross Saltire*.

The *Tau Cross* (4) is like the Latin Cross except that it has no upper arm. It is traditionally the cross used by Moses to lift up the serpent in the wilderness, thus making it a cross of penitence and prophecy.

The *Cross Patée* (patay) (5) is a Greek Cross with arms curving outward from a narrow center to a broad straight or curved end.

The *Cross Alisée Patée* (6) is a cross inscribed within a circle.

The *Maltese Cross* (7) has arms shaped like four spearheads, each arm pointing to the center and terminating at the broad end in two points.

[1] F. R. Webber, *Church Symbolism* (Cleveland, Ohio: J. H. Jansen, 1938), is a good book for church symbols in general. Lucy Vaughan Hayden Mackrille, *Church Embroidery and Church Vestments*, 2d ed. (Chevy Chase, Md.: Cathedral Studios, 1947); and Hinda M. Hands, *Church Needlework* (London: Faith Press, 1920), are very useful in designing symbols for embroidery work.

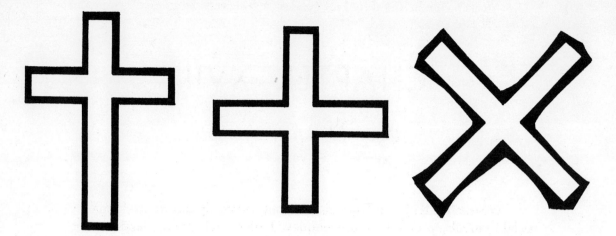

1. Latin Cross   2. Greek Cross   3. St. Andrew's Cross

4. Tau Cross   5. Cross Patée   6. Cross Alisée Patée

7. Maltese Cross   8. Cross Fleuri   9. Passion Cross

The resulting eight outer points symbolize the regeneration of man and also the eight Beatitudes.

The *Cross Fleuri* (8) has arms terminating in three petals. It is one of the most beautiful decorative crosses.

The *Passion Cross* (9) is a cross whose ends are pointed. It symbolizes the sufferings of our Lord and is suitable for Lent, especially Good Friday.

The *Easter Cross* (10) is a white Latin Cross with Easter lilies twined around it.

The *Anchor Cross* (11) is made by combining an anchor and a cross. It is a symbol of Christian hope.

The $\overline{\text{IHC}}$ (12) is a monogram of the holy name Jesus from the Greek IHCOYC. The $\overline{\text{IHS}}$ is a corrupted form of it.

The $\overline{\text{XPC}}$ (13) is a monogram of Christ from the Greek XPICTOC.

The $\overline{\text{XP}}$ (14), pronounced Chi rho, is also a monogram of Christ made up of only the first two Greek letters.

The $\overline{\text{IHC}}$, $\overline{\text{XPC}}$, and $\overline{\text{XP}}$ should have a line above them to show that they are abbreviations.

The INRI (15) is made up of the initial letters of the words which were placed on the cross of Christ, *Iesus Nazarenus Rex Iudaeorum,* meaning "Jesus of Nazareth, King of the Jews." In embroidery work it is usually surrounded by a crown of thorns.

The *Alpha and Omega* (16), the first and the last letters of the Greek alphabet, refer to Christ as the Eternal One. "I am the Alpha and Omega, the beginning and the ending, saith the Lord" (Rev. 1:8). The Alpha and Omega must, therefore, always be used in connection with some symbol of Christ, or else it will be meaningless.

The *Agnus Dei* (17), the Latin for Lamb of God, is one of the most ancient symbols of our Lord. The lamb ought to be conventional rather than realistic. It must be crowned with the three-rayed nimbus, showing that it is a symbol of divinity. The Agnus Dei is shown carrying the banner of victory, or reclining on the Book of Seven Seals, or standing upon a hill from which flow the four rivers of Paradise, signifying the Four Gospels. The Agnus Dei carrying the banner of victory is particularly suitable for the Easter paraments.

The *Fish* is probably the oldest symbol of Christ. The conventionalized form of the fish is the *Vesica,* or *Vesica Piscis* (18). In times of persecution the early Christians had to go underground. In order to identify themselves to one another, they would draw the sign of a fish. Why a fish? The Greek word for fish is IXΘΥΣ. The letters IXΘΥΣ are the initial letters of words which mean, "Jesus Christ, God's Son, Savior."

I — Ἰησοῦς = Jesus
X — Χριστός = Christ
Θ — Θεοῦ = **God's**
Υ — Υἱός = Son
Σ — Σωτήρ = Savior

The sign of the fish identified a person as a Christian.

10. Easter Cross

11. Anchor Cross

12

13

14. Chi-Rho

15

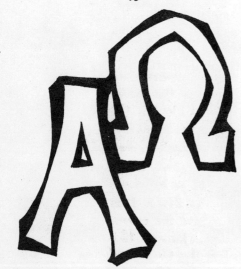

16. Alpha and Omega

17. Agnus Dei

18. Vesica

When three *Vesicas* (the conventionalized fish) are combined, they form the *Triquetra* (19). The Triquetra is a symbol of the Holy Trinity. The three Vesicas illustrate the Three Persons, expressing their equality in the equal Vesicas, their eternity in the continuous line which forms the Triquetra, their indivisibility in the interweaving of the line, and their unity in the triangular form of the Triquetra. This is a very interesting and decorative symbol.

The *Five-pointed Star* (20) is a Messianic symbol, based on the prophecy, "There shall come a Star out of Jacob" (Num. 24:17). It is therefore a very good symbol for the Advent paraments. It is also a proper symbol for the Epiphany, or the manifestation of our Lord to the Gentiles. It is not, however, a Christmas star, because the Christmas scene and the Epiphany scene are separate and distinct. The Magi did not come to the manger at the birth of Christ, but to a house sometime later (Matt. 2:1-11). Christmas itself is not associated with a star.

The *Pelican in Her Piety* (21) is a very widely used symbol of our Lord's atonement. The pelican is shown plucking open her breast and feeding her young with her own lifeblood. So our Lord shed His own lifeblood to give us life and salvation. He feeds us with His blood in the Sacrament of the Altar. This is a fine symbol for use in Passiontide and for the Holy Communion linens.

The *Fleur-de-Lis* (22) is a conventionalized lily and a symbol of the Virgin Mary, the human nature of Christ, and the Annunciation. It is a very popular, interesting, and decorative design.

The *Vine and Branches* (23), is another common and very decorative symbol. It refers to Christ as the Vine and the believers as the branches (John 15:1). Its use on the paraments for the Trinity season and for the Holy Communion linens is most appropriate.

The *Rose of Sharon* (24) is a symbol of the promised Messiah, based on the prophecy, "I am the rose of Sharon and the lily of the valleys" (Song of Solomon 2:1). It is used in a conventionalized form and may be combined with the five-pointed star. With or without the star, it is a good symbol for Advent paraments.

The *Easter Lily* (25) is an exquisite symbol of our Lord's resurrection. It is therefore one of the many familiar symbols seen on the white paraments. It is also a picture of our resurrection to eternal life. As the lily bulb is planted in the ground and from it comes forth a beautiful lily, so through the resurrection of Christ, our dead and buried bodies shall rise to life and glory.

The *Crown* (26) is a symbol of Christ's kingly office. "Be ye lifted up, ye everlasting doors, and the King of glory shall come in" (Ps. 24:7). It is also a symbol of our victory through Christ. "He shall receive the crown of life which the Lord hath promised to them that love Him" (James 1:12). The crown is often combined with a Latin Cross, called the *Cross and Crown*. This signifies that all who bear their crosses in this life as Christians will receive the crown of glory in the life to come.

The *Equilateral Triangle* (27) is one of the oldest symbols of the

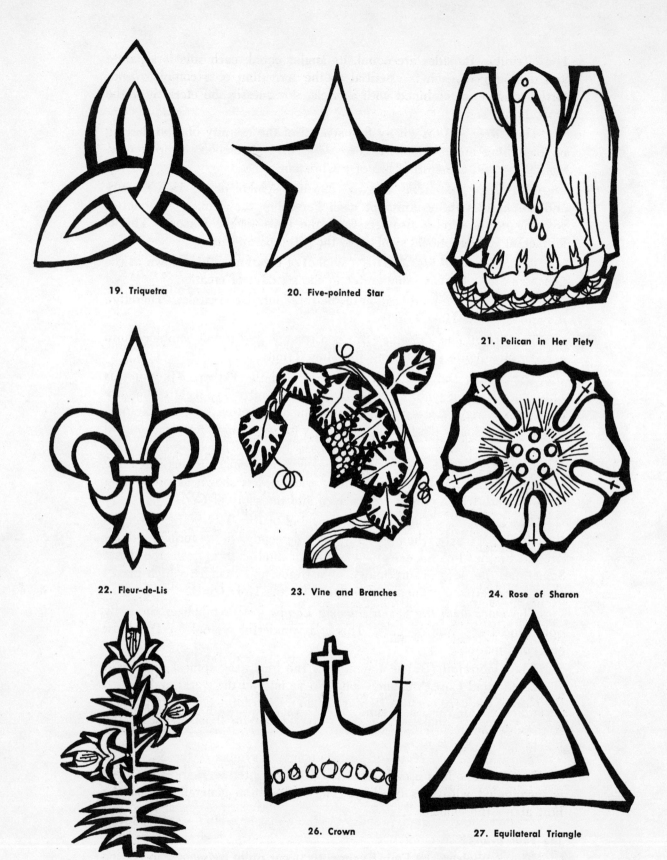

19. Triquetra

20. Five-pointed Star

21. Pelican in Her Piety

22. Fleur-de-Lis

23. Vine and Branches

24. Rose of Sharon

25. Easter Lily

26. Crown

27. Equilateral Triangle

Holy Trinity. Its sides are equal, its angles equal; each side is separate and distinct, yet each is essential to the formation of a complete unit. If the triangle is combined with a circle, it witnesses the eternity of the Holy Trinity.

The *Circle* (28) is a very fine symbol of the eternity of God, having no beginning and no end. It also symbolizes perfection, completeness, continuity, and the eternal life of a Christian.

The *Three Interlacing Circles* (29) is a symbol of the Holy Trinity and emphasizes the eternity of each Person of the Trinity. The interweaving of the circles also sets forth the unity of the Persons. This is a graceful and devotional symbol for the green paraments.

The *Six-pointed Star* (30) is a symbol of creation and is known as the *Creator's Star*. The six points refer to the six days of creation.

The *Trefoil* is a modification of the three interlaced circles. Therefore it symbolizes the Holy Trinity.

The *Trefoil and Triangle* (31) is a triangle and trefoil combined into a decorative figure symbolizing the Holy Trinity.

The *Manus Dei* (32) is a symbol of God the Father. The name is Latin for "hand of God." The right hand of God refers to His almighty power. "His right hand and His holy arm hath gotten Him the victory" (Ps. 98:1). Usually the hand is pictured with the thumb, first, and second fingers extended and the other two fingers closed. This represents God's blessings. The Manus Dei is surrounded with a circular nimbus and three rays to indicate the Deity. Sometimes the hand is shown as proceeding from a cloud, which emphasizes heaven and the glory of God.

The *Descending Dove* (33) is a symbol of the Holy Spirit, based on the baptism of Christ when the Holy Spirit descended in the form of a dove. Around the head of the dove is a triradiant nimbus to indicate the deity. Sometimes the dove is surrounded by a trefoil and triangle, which makes a very decorative and meaningful figure for the Holy Ghost.

The *Dove with the Seven Burning Lamps* (34) symbolizes the Holy Spirit and His sevenfold gifts. This is a wonderful symbol for Pentecost and confirmation.

The *Quatrefoil* (35) is a symbol of the four geographical directions. It calls to mind Christ's commission, "Go ye into all the world and preach the Gospel to every creature" (Mark 16:15). It is formed from four interwoven circles and makes a fine decorative border for the Holy Bible, the Dove, and the Rose.

The *Chalice and Host* (36) is the common symbol of the Sacrament of the Altar. The host usually has the INRI imprinted on it and sometimes is surrounded with rays of glory. The composition generally shows the host above the chalice.

The Four Evangelists

The symbols of the Four Evangelists occur quite frequently in church needlework. They are the winged creatures referred to in the Bible, both in Ezekiel and Revelation. Sometimes only the head and wings are pictured

28. Circle   29. Three Interlacing Circles   30. Six-pointed Star

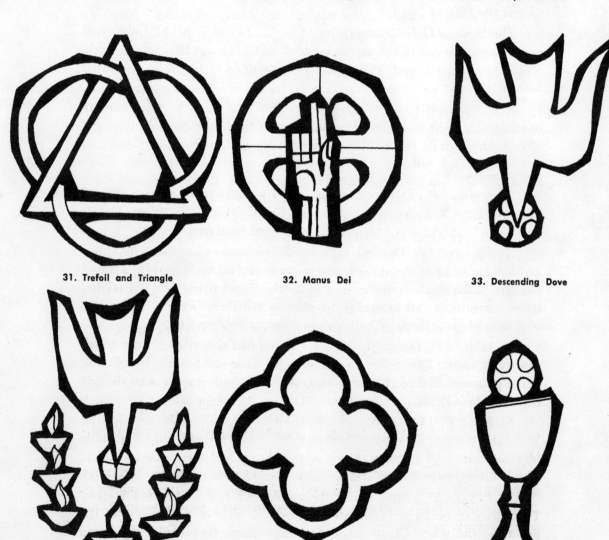

31. Trefoil and Triangle   32. Manus Dei   33. Descending Dove

34. Dove with the Seven Burning Lamps   35. Quatrefoil   36. Chalice and Host

and at other times the whole body. The head always has a nimbus. When they are arranged around a symbol or emblem of Christ, St. John is on the left on top and St. Matthew is on the right; St. Mark on the bottom left and St. Luke on the right.

The *Winged Man* (37) stands for St. Matthew. This is probably the case because the Gospel According to St. Matthew opens with the human ancestry of our Lord and in general stresses the manhood of Christ.

The *Winged Lion* (38) stands for St. Mark. The Gospel According to St. Mark opens with a description of St. John the Baptist, who speaks of himself as the voice of one crying in the wilderness. That this should be associated with the voice of a lion is quite natural. St. Mark also emphasizes the resurrection of Christ. The resurrection declares the ability of Christ to overcome all His enemies, which reminds one of the lion, who is the king of beasts.

The *Winged Ox* (39) stands for St. Luke. In his gospel St. Luke gives an extensive account of the sacrificial death of Christ and His atoning work. Since the ox was a sacrificial animal, the sacrifice of Christ is associated with that of an ox.

The *Eagle* (40) stands for St. John. The eagle flies higher than any other bird, and the Gospel of St. John soars to heights greater than the other Gospels in its theology of Christ.

The Apostles

St. Andrew (41), November 30, has the emblem of a cross shaped like the letter X, called the St. Andrew Cross. This is the type of cross on which St. Andrew is believed to have been martyred.

St. Thomas (42), December 21, has the emblem of a carpenter's square and a spear. The carpenter's square refers to the tradition that St. Thomas built a church in India with his own hands. The vertical spear is related to his martyrdom. He is said to have been shot down with an arrow and was then pierced through by a pagan priest with a spear.

St. John (43), December 27, has the emblem of a chalice from which a serpent rises. This refers to an attempt made on his life by offering him a poisoned chalice. St. John, however, is the only apostle who did not die a martyr's death.

St. Matthias (44), February 24, who was chosen to take the place of Judas the traitor, has the emblem of a Bible and a battle-axe. The Bible identifies him as a great preacher of the Word, and the battle-axe refers to his martyrdom. He is said to have been stoned and then beheaded.

St. Philip (45), May 1, has the emblem of two loaves and a cross. The loaves of bread are associated with the miracle of the feeding of the five thousand when Christ asked St. Philip where they could buy bread enough to feed so many people. The cross refers to his martyrdom. He was scourged, stoned, and finally crucified.

St. James the Less (46), May 1, has the emblem of a saw. Tradition says that he was pushed off a pinnacle of the temple. Although he was

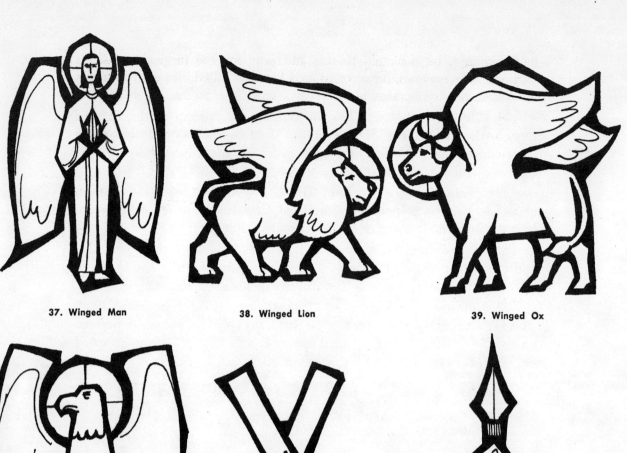

37. Winged Man   38. Winged Lion   39. Winged Ox

40. Eagle   41. St. Andrew   42. St. Thomas

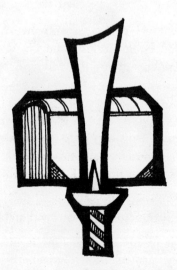

43. St. John   44. St. Matthias   45. St. Philip

badly injured, he managed to rise and pray for the forgiveness of his enemies. The enemies, however, stoned him and killed him with a fuller's bat. Then they desecrated his body by sawing it in pieces.

St. Peter (47), June 29, has the well-known emblem of the Crossed Keys or the Keys Saltire. The reference is, of course, to our Lord's statement concerning the Office of the Keys.

St. James the Elder (48), July 25, has the emblem of three escalloped shells, two above and one below. This is a symbol of pilgrimage, others of which, like the pilgrim's staff and hat, are also emblems of St. James, who died as a martyr under Herod Agrippa. (Acts 12:2)

St. Bartholomew (49), August 24, has the emblem of the open Bible and the flaying knife. The Bible refers to his great faith in the Word of God, and the flaying knife to the manner of his martyrdom.

St. Matthew (50), September 21, has the emblem of three money bags. This is a reference to the fact that he was a tax collector before he became an apostle. He is said to have died as a martyr in Ethiopia, being crucified on a Tau Cross and having his head cut off with a battle-axe.

St. Jude (51), October 28, also called Thaddæus and Lebbæus, has the emblem of a sailship with a mast in the shape of a cross. He and St. Simon are said to have traveled by ship on their missionary journeys.

St. Simon (52), October 28, also called Zelotes, has the emblem of a fish resting on the closed end of a Bible. This shows that through the power of the Word of God he was a great fisher of men. According to tradition, he and St. Jude met a martyr's death together while on a missionary journey in Persia.

St. Paul (53)—Conversion, January 25; St. Peter and St. Paul, June 29—has the familiar emblem of an open Bible with the Sword of the Spirit. This is a reference to the words of the Epistle of St. Paul to the Ephesians: "Take . . . the sword of the Spirit, which is the Word of God." (Eph. 6:17)

Lutheran Symbols

Luther's Coat of Arms (54) is a cross on a heart, reposing on a Messianic Rose, and surrounded by a circle. John G. Morris, *Quaint Sayings and Doings Concerning Luther*,[2] gives the following description:

> It was of a circular form, with a white rose in the center, on which there was a heart, with a black cross upon it. The whole was enclosed by a gold ring, with these words around it: In patientia suavitas, that is "in patience, sweetness." On the reverse was found this inscription:

> Des Christen Herz auf Rosen geht,
> **Wenn's mitten unterm Kreutze steht.**

> "The Christian's heart on roses lies,
> When at the cross it moans and sighs."

Luther's own account of his coat of arms is given in a letter to Lazarus Spengler, government clerk at Nüremberg.

[2] Quoted in the *American Lutheran*, XIII (June 1930), 15. See also "Description of Luther's Coat of Arms" (editorial), *American Lutheran*, XIII (June 1930), 15.

46. St. James the Less

47. St. Peter

48. St. James the Elder

49. St. Bartholomew

50. St. Matthew

51. St. Jude

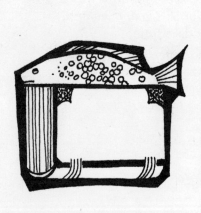

52. St. Simon

53. St. Paul

54. Luther's Coat of Arms

Grace and Peace in Christ!

Honorable Sir and Respected Friend:

As you desire to know whether my seal is correct, I will give you my first thoughts, for gold company, which I intended to have engraven upon my seal, as expressive of my theology. The first thing was to be a cross (black) within the heart, having its natural color, to put me in mind that faith in Christ crucified saved us. "For with the heart man believeth unto righteousness." Now although the cross is black, mortified, and intended to cause pain, yet does it not change the color of the heart, does not corrupt nature, that is, does not kill but keeps alive. "For the just shall live by faith," but by faith in the Savior. But this heart is fixed upon the center of a white rose, to show that faith causes joy and consolation and peace, not as the world gives peace and joy. For this reason the rose is white, and not red, because white is the color of all angels and blessed spirits. This rose, moreover, is fixed in a sky-colored ground, to denote that such joy of faith in the spirit is but an earnest and beginning of heavenly joy to come, as anticipated and held by hope, though not yet revealed. And around this ground-base is a golden ring, to signify that such bliss in heaven is endless, and more precious than all joys and treasures, since gold is the best and most precious metal.

Christ, our dear Lord, be with your spirit unto eternal life. Amen.

Concordia (55) is a symbol of the agreement and harmony in matters of doctrine and practice set forth in the Confessions of the Lutheran Church, which are contained in the Book of Concord of 1580. It consists of Luther's Coat of Arms imposed on a harp. The harp represents harmony and the coat of arms refers to the Lutheran Church.

55. Concordia

CHAPTER XIX

About Helpful Books, Magazines, and Visual Aids

Books

Beck, Victor E., and Paul M. Lindberg. *A Book of Advent.* Rock Island: Augustana Press, 1958.

Candwell, Irene. *Flowers in Church.* New York: Morehouse-Barlow Co., 1942.

Conway, J. Gregory. *Flowers, East-West.* New York: A. A. Knopp, 1940.

The Crib. London: A. R. Mowbray & Co., n. d.

Dearmer, Percy. *The Ornaments of the Ministers.* London: A. R. Mowbray & Co., 1920.

De Candole, Henry. *Lent with the Church.* New York: Morehouse-Barlow Co., 1952.

Diggs, Dorothy C. *A Working Manual for Altar Guilds.* New York: Morehouse-Barlow Co., 1950.

Fitts, Frederic W. *The Altar.* Boston: Anglican Society, 1940.

Flueler, Augusta. *Paramente.* Zurich: NZN-Verlag, 1949. Written in German, but very valuable as an expression of modern ideas about vestments.

Frank, V. C. *The Rainbow in My Church.* Milwaukee: Northwestern Publishing House, 1957.

General Rubrics, a reprint from *The Lutheran Liturgy.* St. Louis: Concordia Publishing House, 1955.

Griffith, Helen Stuart. *The Sign Language of Our Faith.* Washington, D. C.: Washington Cathedral, 1950.

Hands, Hinda M. *Church Needlework.* London: The Faith Press, 1920. Available in U. S. A. from Morehouse-Barlow Co., New York.

Home and Garden Bulletin No. 62 lists methods of removing stains of all kinds from fabrics. Write to the Superintendent of Documents, U. S. Department of Agriculture, Washington, D. C.

Horn III, Edward T. *The Christian Year.* Philadelphia: Muhlenberg Press, 1957.

Horn III, Edward T. *The Church at Worship.* Philadelphia: Muhlenberg Press, 1960.

Koenker, Ernest B. *Worship in Word and Sacrament.* St. Louis: Concordia Publishing House, 1959.

Kretzmann, A. R. *Symbols.* St. Louis: Concordia Publishing House, 1944.

Kunkle, Howard R. *A Manual for Altar Guilds.* Columbus: Wartburg Press, 1947.

Lang, Paul H. D. *Ceremony and Celebration.* St. Louis: Concordia Publishing House, 1965.

Lang, Paul H. D. *Church Ushering.* St. Louis: Concordia Publishing House, 1946.

Lang, Paul H. D. *Lutheran Church Worship*. New York: American Lutheran Publicity Bureau, 1954. A tract.

Lang, Paul H. D. *Questions Often Asked by a Newcomer into a Lutheran Church*. Brooklyn: Una Sancta Press, 1952. This booklet answers such questions as: "Why is the chalice used in Holy Communion?" "Why Communion every Sunday?" "Why are vestments worn by the minister?"

Lang, Paul H. D. *The Lutheran Order of Services*. St. Louis: Concordia Publishing House, 1952.

Lenten Devotions for Use in Evangelical Lutheran Churches. Printed by The Mary-Martha Guild of the Lutheran Chapel of the Incarnation, Pompton Lakes, N. J., 1950.

Lornell, Ruby. *Lift Up Your Hearts*. Rock Island: Augustana Book Concern, 1955.

McArthur, A. Alan. *Evolution of the Christian Year*. London: SCM Press, 1953.

McCance, Murray. *Sacred Vestments in the Classical Tradition*. Ontario: St. Thomas, 1959. Good illustrations of contemporary styles of vestments.

McClinton, Katharine M. *Flower Arrangement in the Church*. New York: Morehouse-Barlow Co., 1945.

McClinton, Katharine M., and Isabel W. Squier. *Good Housekeeping in the Church*. New York: Morehouse-Barlow Co., 1953.

Mackrille, Lucy V. *A Handbook for Altar Guilds*. Washington, D. C.: Cathedral Studio, 1931.

Menges, David A. *The Altar Guild*. Philadelphia: Muhlenberg Press, 1944.

Norris, Herbert. *Church Vestments*. London: J. M. Dent & Son, 1949.

Paschal Candle and the Easter Vigil. Brooklyn: Una Sancta, 1957.

Perry, Edith Weir. *An Altar Guild Manual*. New York: Morehouse-Barlow, 1946.

Piepkorn, A. C. *Worship and the Sacraments*. St. Louis: Concordia Publishing House, 1955. This booklet gives the official Lutheran position as stated in the Lutheran Confessions in the Book of Concord. Very important.

Reed, Luther D. *The Lutheran Liturgy*. Philadelphia: Muhlenberg Press, 1947.

Reed, Luther D. *Worship*. Philadelphia: Muhlenberg Press, 1961.

Reinertsen, Peter A. *Acolytes and Altar Guilds*. Rock Island: Augustana Press, 1960.

Rockwell, F. F. *Flower Arrangement*. New York: Macmillan Co., 1940.

Roulin, E. A. *Vestments and Vesture*. Westminster: The Newman Press, 1950.

Runge, Kenneth E. *Advent. The Paschal Candle. Holy Confirmation. The Lutheran Funeral*. Detroit: Zion Lutheran Church.

Ruoss, G. Martin. *The Acolyte*. Mechanicsburg: private publication, 1959.

Ruoss, G. Martin. *An Altar Guild Workbook*. Mechanicsburg: private publication, 1955.

Ruoss, G. Martin. *A Church Tour*. New York: Greenwich Book Publishing Co., 1957.

Smart, Henry. *The Altar*. New York: Morehouse-Barlow Co., 1950.

Strodach, Paul Zeller. *The Church Year*. Philadelphia: Muhlenberg Press, 1924.

Strodach, Paul Zeller. *A Manual on Worship*. Philadelphia: Muhlenberg Press, 1946.

Trexeler, Jr., Charles D. *Advent in the Home*. Brooklyn: Una Sancta Press, 1959.

Webber, F. R. *Church Symbolism*. Cleveland: J. H. Jansen Publishing Co., 1937.

Webber, F. R. *The Small Church*. Cleveland: J. H. Jansen Publishing Co., 1939.

Weiser, Francis X. *Handbook of Christian Feasts and Customs*. New York: Harcourt, Brace and Co., 1958.

Weitzler, Robert, and Helen Huntington. *Seasons and Symbols*. Minneapolis: Augsburg Publishing House, 1960.

Magazines

Response. Lutheran Society for Worship, Music and the Arts, 2100 Riverside Ave., Minneapolis, Minn. 55404.

Una Sancta. 195 Maujer St., Brooklyn, N. Y. 11206.

Visual Aids

Write to the National Cathedral Association in Washington, D. C., for a series of slides on altar guild work. Included is a set on flower arrangement.

Duties of the Altar Guild. A color filmstrip produced as a companion piece for this manual. St. Louis: Concordia Publishing House.

O Worship the Lord. Color filmstrip with record. St. Louis: Concordia Publishing House.

Symbols of the Church. A set of six filmstrips and three records. The individual titles are: Symbols of Faith, Symbols of the Cross, Lost Symbols, Symbols of the House of God, Symbols of the New Testament, Symbols of the Old Testament. St. Louis: Concordia Publishing House.

Colored slides on *"Altar Preparation."* Covenant Altar Guild, c/o Mrs. Arlene Rapp, 19000 Libby Road, Maple Heights, Ohio 44137

The Order of the Holy Communion. A filmstrip by Luthercraft Productions, New York, N. Y. St. Louis: Concordia Publishing House.

Lutheran Liturgy in Slow Motion. American Lutheran Publicity Bureau, 315 Park Ave. South, New York, N. Y. 10010.

Our Christian Symbols. A filmstrip by Frederick Rest. The Christian Education Press, 1505 Race St., Philadelphia, Pa. 19102.

Morehouse-Barlow Co., New York, Chicago, and San Francisco, has filmstrips on many subjects, such as: The Holy Eucharist, The Vestments of the Church, The Sacred Vessels, Care of the Sanctuary, Christian Symbolism, The House of God.

INDEX